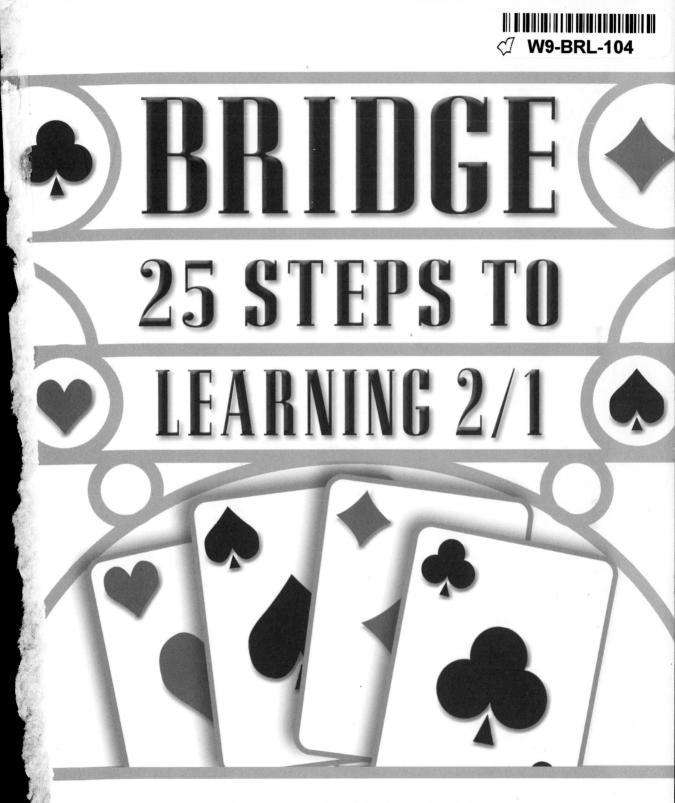

BRIDGE
25 STEPS TO
LEARNING 2/1

PAUL THURSTON

BRIDGE

25 STEPS TO LEARNING 2/1

MASTER POINT PRESS • TORONTO

Master Point Press

331 Douglas Ave.
Toronto, Ontario Canada
M5M 1H2
(416) 781-0351 Fax (416) 781-1831
Internet www.masterpointpress.com

Canadian Cataloguing in Publication Data

Thurston, Paul
Bridge: 25 steps to learning 2/1

ISBN 1-894154-46-0

1. Contract bridge — Bidding. I. Title:
GV1282.4.T48 2002   795.41'52   C2001-904150-0

Editor	Ray Lee
Cover and Interior design	Olena S. Sullivan
Interior format and copyediting	Deanna Bourassa

Printed and bound in Canada by Webcom Canada Ltd.

2 3 4 5 6 7   06 05 04

F O R E W O R D

Paul Thurston is a true believer. If one can imagine writing about a card game from the heart, he's achieved that state of grace in this, his first book, an introduction to state-of-the-art mainstream North American bidding.

The methods and ideas that Paul outlines and carefully explains in the pages you are about to read are those he employs himself and teaches his students. When he tells you that you can play Two-over-One with anyone after absorbing what's in this book, he is not simply plugging his pet system. These methods are popular and not difficult to grasp or remember. If they make sense to you, as Paul's guidance is bound to ensure, you'll find that the learning curve is not steep and that you will be up and running in no time at all.

As Paul tells you in the final chapter, this book is only an introduction to Two-over-One and several essential areas will be broached in a second volume. For example, there is nothing in these 25 Steps about notrump openings and only a few words about two-bids, whether weak, strong or conventional. That's because individual choices in these areas are perfectly acceptable and for the most part (notrump range does influence other actions significantly) do not affect the essence of modern Two-over-One bidding.

You may not be smitten with everything you read here or might be unlucky enough to encounter one of the awkward hands for these methods (for example, responder's game-invitational minor one-suiters after a major-suit opening, or a truly unpleasant eleven-count like:

♠ A 6 4   ♥ 5 3   ♦ K Q 7   ♣ Q 5 4 3 2

after a one-diamond opening). However, the systemic building blocks you will find in this book can be adopted selectively. You can choose what parts you like and even tinker with some of the basic structures to suit yourself. While Paul gives you a cohesive system that deals effectively with most high frequency situations and never leaves you floundering (there's always a least-of-evils solution), it's a fact of life that bridge players learn from their own experience and rarely buy everything that's offered without question. That's healthy and positive, especially where conventions or artificial treatments are concerned. The author is realistic about this, too, and throughout the book you will find alternative ideas and caveats worth heeding.

This book moves along. It's an enjoyable read and offers valuable summaries and excellent review problems at the end of each section. You can be playing Two-over-One effectively within a week, and to that end Paul's first book gets the job done. And you'll have fun too, which should be one of the goals of any instructive tome at any level.

Eric Kokish

C O N T E N T S

INTRODUCTION

> ♥ The American system has been called scientific by many writers. A greater misnomer it is impossible to conceive.
> *Criticus.* **Contract Simplicitas.** *1933.*

Just like the language you speak, the language of bridge bidding is constantly evolving and improving. As an adult, you use a more sophisticated version of English than you did as a child; similarly, as you gain more experience at the bridge table, you will probably want to use something more modern than the basic Standard bidding system you were first taught to play.

In this book, I'm going to introduce you to what many believe to be the most effective bidding language for both today and the immediate future. Whether you play our great game in purely social settings, at a club, logged on to your favorite Internet site or on the tournament trail, there will be something for you in these Twenty-Five Steps. No weight loss, spiritual enrichment or fantastic financial gain (sorry!), but you will bid better!

There'll also be some work involved (sorry again!) – you won't be able to slip the book under a pillow and use sleep-osmosis – so let's look at some good reasons for you to take on the job.

1) It's universal

The language we're going to explore together is the Two-over-One system, a relatively modern approach that has been in the developmental stages for something on the order of forty years. As a departure from Standard American, this system traces its roots to American expert Alvin Roth, undoubtedly the most original thinker in bridge since the glory days of Ely Culbertson.

Just as with real spoken languages, however, the 'newness' of this approach comes from developments in the trenches — the trials and errors of inventive players taking on, shaping and refining the elements they find beneficial.

In more recent times, Two-over-One has been primarily shaped and written about by a disparate troika of American theorists-players-teachers – Marty Bergen, Mike Lawrence and Max Hardy. These three have done yeoman service in trying to make the bidding practices and theories of expert players accessible to everyone.

Today, Two-over-One is no longer reserved for just the experts — players at all levels of skill and experience can and do profitably adopt and use this approach. Indeed, a semi-scientific survey I recently conducted of those playing on three separate Internet sites found about 40% of the players from no less than twenty-one different countries playing a version of Two-over-One.

That so many players in all corners of the world have at least a passable working knowledge of Two-over-One is now one of its greatest virtues — it has wide acceptance and whether or not you decide to play the system yourself, acquiring a working knowledge of it will at the very least make you better equipped to cope with many opponents.

2) It's familar

As an offspring of Standard American, Two-over-One will not cause a major shock to your comfort zone. If Standard American is your bridge birth language, acquiring fluency in Two-over-One will be more akin to an English-speaking student learning French or Italian than attempting to master an exotic language like Mandarin or Swahili.

There will be much vocabulary and syntax shared with Standard American, whether you learned your basics from the writings of Charles Goren, Dorothy Truscott or Audrey Grant. And if, like the vast majority, you've picked up 'how to bid' along the way from a variety of sources, 'speaking' Two-over-One will smooth out some of the rough edges of that 'street' bidding.

Just to underline what I'm saying here, let me point out that there's nothing in this book about opening 1NT or opening two-bids. That's because whatever you do right now is just fine. I'm assuming you play a 15-17 notrump, but what you want to play after that is entirely up to you — Stayman, 2-way or 4-way transfers, Baron, and all the rest. Similarly, if you like Multi 2♦, or two-under preempts, or simple weak two-bids, don't change a thing. Similarly, your methods for handling auctions where the opponents have opened the bidding can remain unaltered. The only parts of your system that are going to change at all are those that involve your side opening the bidding with one of a suit — and many of those will still be very recognizable.

3) It's adoptable and adaptable

What you are going to encounter in our Twenty-Five Steps is virtually 100% adoptable for immediate and successful use. Okay, there will be a mild adjustment period during which some confusion (translation: bad results and occasional headaches) will occur, but you'll get over that stage easily enough.

About 80% of what you'll learn is based on what I've been playing in a very successful twenty-year partnership with Rick Delogu. This language has also passed the acid test of the several hundred students I've been fortunate enough to teach — casualties have been few and successes many.

Further, one of the great virtues of this approach is that you and the partner of your choice can tinker with it, adding or subtracting as you see fit, without doing serious damage to the fundamental concepts. Don't worry — I'll warn you if there are areas where such tinkering has explosive potential!

In the end, whether you graft on elements of the Twenty-Five Steps to a different systemic approach or embrace them totally, you will profit from the exercise of working through them.

4) It's effective

A review of reports from most championship events, teams or pairs, will generally reveal that the trophies are won and lost in the arena of game and slam bidding. Classical Standard American has often been found wanting in this category over the years, its proponents having been bested time after time by players using various Forcing Club systems.

Without being a totally radical departure from its North American antecedents, Two-over-One is a refined approach that addresses and corrects many of the weaknesses in Standard that have been made apparent in top-flight competition. The ease and accuracy of bidding games and slams is much improved, particularly in the major suits.

However, this improvement is not just for Internationalists. Have you ever stopped in a partscore only to find that making enough tricks to have earned a game bonus was duck soup? 'Don't worry, partner, we couldn't have bid that – the hands just happened to fit perfectly.' Have you ever heard or said that?

Twenty-one point games or twenty-four point slams are not only often makable but also biddable — and not just by Italian experts or your local club's riverboat gamblers! By the time we're done, you're going to be bidding to consistently better and more rewarding contracts than you previously thought possible.

5) It's fun!

Bridge is a game! It's meant to be played! Sure, there's a scoring system involved so we all want to do our best, but if there's no fun, what's the use? This part you'll have to take on faith, for a little while at least, but rest assured that Two-over-One can be a fun system to use. For starters, one of the biggest bugaboos about learning how to bid better is often 'there's too much to remember'. Yes, I will ask you to learn and remember some new bidding concepts and conventions but there will be a consistent logic to it all; understanding will be far more important than remembering — and easier, too!

Many players like at least some 'science' and discipline in their bidding, if only to rein in their occasionally overexuberant partner. Creative thinking in a structured framework will be our goal.

Do you currently take a lot of tricks in the bidding? No, we aren't going to change the way the game is played but you will soon find yourself making comments like 'I knew how the play would go before dummy came down' — thanks to our new approach. That's fun!

Harassing the opponents in the bidding with little or no risk to your side can also be a source of enjoyment and you'll find lots of opportunities to do just that in the Two-over-One approach.

And, of course, what it's all about — improved communications with that person you've chosen to sit across the table from — will inevitably lead to superior results — and that's really fun!

COUNT
YOUR POINTS

♥ Bear in mind that everything you have learned about Bidding and Valuation Methods need not be unlearned. **The Official System of Contract Bridge.** *1931.*

After twenty-five-plus years of teaching beginners how to get started playing this amazing game of ours, I've come to realize that we – teachers, writers, experienced players – make learning bridge much more difficult than it needs to be. Initiation into a secret society may be enhanced by arcane ceremonies or incantations, but learning to play a game should be easier than this one seems to be.

Without doubt, one of the places we make it difficult for new players for no good reason is in separating cardplay from bidding. This separation occurs most noticeably when we evaluate the strength of a hand and try to express it in the bidding. As you know, a good bridge hand is one that, on its own or in conjunction with partner's assets, will take lots of tricks. Why, then, is learning to bid all about counting points?

How did it all start?

A gentleman named Bryant McCampbell first introduced the ancestor of the virtually universally used modern point-count system way back in 1915.

Milton Work added some refinements in the 20s (perhaps contributing to both the 'Roaring' epithet and eventually the Crash) and his legacy, The Work Point Count, was eventually adopted and turned into a massive popular success by Charles Goren (and to a slightly lesser extent Fred Karpin), starting in the 1950s.

Goren's genius was definitely in popularizing and marketing bridge and in order that his product portfolio could sensibly include the Goren Count, some further refinements were needed. Devising these additions and modifications fell to Torontonian William Anderson, an actuary by profession.

And therein lies the rub! Without meaning any ill will to future generations of bridge players, a lawyer (Goren) and an actuary (Anderson) were responsible for a tool (the Goren Point Count) that was decidedly more suitable for marketing the game of bridge than for playing it.

Hands up anyone who hasn't gone through the trauma of a partnership squabble over whether a hand should be valued as twelve or thirteen or maybe even fourteen points because 'according to Goren' you should count:

> **For an Ace = 4 points**
> **For a King = 3 points**
> **For a Queen = 2 points**
> **For a Jack = 1 point**

But don't forget to add:

> **For a void = 3 points**
> **A singleton = 2 points**
> **A doubleton = 1 point**

But you may have to make these adjustments:

> **Unguarded honors = minus 1 point**
> **Raising with 3 trumps = minus 1 point**
> **4-3-3-3 distribution = minus 1 point**

However, if you're responder and planning on showing support for partner, some of this changes, such that:

> **For a void = +5 points**
> **For a singleton = +3 points**
> **For a doubleton = +1 point**

Ad nauseam, ad infinitum!

This is the original 'short-suit' counting method for distributional points – many teachers today prefer an alternative but similar process that involves counting extra cards in long suits. Clearly, however, what started out as a simple yardstick for hand evaluation has become amazingly complex in the search for accuracy.

While I was teaching my first large class of beginners many years ago, one young lady whom I had guesstimated to be quite bright dramatically illustrated the sense of pain and futility this point-counting process can occasion in people trying to master it.

With only the 4-3-2-1 high card points chart and the 3-2-1 distributional points chart on the blackboard as guidelines, I gave the students four sample hands to count, asking them to tell me when they got an answer. Not only was my 'promising' student the last of the forty-odd to arrive at an answer, she got the wrong total on each of the first three. So much for her career as a player!

While they all counted the fourth hand, I decided to look over her shoulder to perhaps get an inkling as to why she was having such a problem with this 'simple' exercise. As she mentally plowed through the minefield of calculations, here's what I saw fanned in her hand:

♠A ♦A ♥K ♦Q ♣J ♥J ♦J ♦10 ♠8 ♥5 ♦5 ♥3 ♦3

You try to count that hand!

Enough!

Counting points is never going to be totally done away with, at least until some new millennium genius invents a superior method that at least seems as easy. However, the pre-auction phase of counting points doesn't have to be so complicated as to require a pocket calculator or, for the traditionalists, an abacus. Let's not wear ourselves out before the bidding even starts!

For now, just do it this way:

For each Ace = count 4 points

For each King = count 3 points

For each Queen = count 2 points

For each Jack = count 1 point.

This is the way real bridge players count points. It's easier! It's faster! It won't create distortions in the bidding! No, you won't be a bad person if you discard the baggage handed down by generations of actuaries who've masqueraded as bridge players. It will truly be as easy as 4-3-2-1 ! (Well, for now, anyway!) Oh, and by the way, you may sort your cards into suits first!

WE'LL OPEN THE BIDDING – WON'T WE?

> ♥ The opening bid of one is bed-rock – the foundation on which the contract is erected. Hence it must be strong and dependable. **The Official System of Contract Bridge.** *1931.*

As the foundation for all the bidding that follows, this step defining what we're showing with an opening bid may very well be the most important part of the system.

Two-over-One, like its Standard American ancestors, is essentially a natural approach to bidding. This starts with opening bids that promise a specified range of strength, usually measured by the 4-3-2-1 point scale (hereafter called HCP for high card points) we've just re-learned to count. The opening bid also identifies certain suit-length features of our hand. The minimum guarantees of both HCP and suit lengths are described further as the bidding develops.

BY THE WAY

Although Italy's Leaning Tower of Pisa has been a long-term success with a doubtful foundation, your bidding will be better with a firm foundation – unless you'd like to have your auctions displayed so that generations of tourists can admire the eccentricities of your bidding.

Just as the amount of goods our dollar buys has been decreasing over the last twenty years, so too the standards for opening bids have been creeping ever downwards. However, we do need to be on the same page for our discussions on bidding so let's 'set the bar' at a level we can all live with.

1. We will open a one-bid with all hands containing 12-20 HCP. (Some exceptional hands with great suit length in this range of strength will be treated differently, but they are rare – stay tuned!)

2. Additionally, we will open a one-bid with some hands with 11 HCP if we also have a good quality 6-card or longer suit (major or minor) or two 'touching' 5-card suits of good quality. (This is all about being prepared to make a rebid – more, a lot more, on this later.)

3. If you'd like a 'quality standard' to apply here, try the 4-point criterion for the time being: a 'good quality' suit has at least 4 HCP in it, with some extra spot-card texture if at the lower end of the range. So, KJ10974 is 'good' while KJ6432 isn't, and AQJ542 (7 HCP) is good while QJ9875 (only 3 HCP) isn't.

4. A further quality control you might like to add for borderline openings has to do with defensive assets. A sensible minimum or even sub-minimum opening bid should contain about two defensive tricks. One Ace is a defensive trick, as is a King-Queen combination.

5. You will be on firm ground in the auction if you reject opening any minimum hand that has two or more serious flaws such as fewer than 12 HCP, poor quality suits or not enough defensive tricks.

BY THE WAY

If this is your first encounter with 'touching' as a bridge term, be advised that it has nothing to do with emotional content. 'Touching' suits are those that are immediately adjacent to one another on the bidding ladder. Thus, hearts & diamonds are touching as are diamonds & clubs and hearts & spades. Perhaps surprisingly, in this context, clubs & spades are also considered touching. In case you haven't figured it out, spades & diamonds and hearts & clubs are the non-touching combinations.

BY THE WAY

Not only is it okay that your 1NT opening may contain a 5-card major, but to fit with the rest of our bidding structure, it is virtually imperative that the 1NT opening be used on these hands. A weak doubleton is also okay. However, we do draw the line somewhere – don't open 1NT with a 5-card major and two unstopped suits. Also, don't open 1NT with an excellent 5-card major and a maximum (17 HCP) hand.

Our armory

Two-over-One is essentially a natural system that features a strong notrump opening and five-card major openings. Let's now look at what we promise with our opening bids from 1♦ through 2NT inclusive.

1. **1♣ or 1♦**   12+ HCP, 3+ cards in the suit bid
2. **1♥ or 1♠**   12+ HCP, 5+ cards in the suit bid
3. **1NT**   15-17 HCP in a balanced hand ('Balanced' means 4-3-3-3, 4-4-3-2 or 5-3-3-2 distribution.)

4. 2♦/2♥/2♠ Natural weak-two bids promising 5-11 HCP and a good quality 6-card suit. You can add your own 'style' here to some extent but try to avoid having a side 4-card major of any quality, especially if your partner hasn't already passed, and please, no 7-card suits!

5. 2♣ Strong, artificial and forcing;

   22+HCP if balanced

   20+HCP if unbalanced – but trick-taking potential will be a factor as well. More later.

6. 2NT 20-21 HCP in a balanced hand; 5-card major perfectly acceptable, even encouraged.

   Some 5-4-2-2 shapes okay, too, as long as the doubletons are strong and the two long suits aren't both majors.

So many choices

There will be occasions when you have to make a choice as to which suit to bid when you open:

1. With 3-3 in the minors (and no 5-card major), open 1♣, regardless of the relative quality of the suits. This is not a 'Short Club' – those are reserved for diminutive golfers! It allows for retaining the greatest possible integrity of our 1♦ opening so that the only time we have as few as three diamonds when we open the suit will be when we have exactly four spades, four hearts, three diamonds and two clubs (4-4-3-2 shape).

2. With 4-4 in the minors (and no 5-card major), open 1♦. This is all about being prepared for your rebid without or (especially) with opponents' interference.

3. For purposes of ease and accuracy of rebids – please accept this on faith for now – you should also open 1♦ with 4-5 distribution in the minors as long as the diamonds are of reasonable quality (the 4 HCP rule can apply here as well). So with

   ♠ 72 ♥ 85 ♦ AQ72 ♣ AQ872

   open 1♦.

4. With 5-5 in any two suits, always open the higher-ranked suit, except when the two suits are spades and clubs; then open:

   1♣ with 12-15 HCP

   1♠ with 16-17 HCP

   1♣ with 18+ HCP

Summary

✓ 1-bids promise 12 HCP (occasional exceptions with 11 HCP).

✓ 1♣ or 1♦ promises 3 cards in the bid suit, with 1♦ usually delivering 4.

✓ 1♥ or 1♠ promises 5 cards in the bid suit.

✓ 1NT promises 15-17 HCP — may have a 5-card major and may have an unstopped suit or weak doubleton.

✓ Holding 4-4 in the minors, usually open 1♦.

✓ Holding 5-5 in any two suits (except spades and clubs), open the higher-ranked; with spades and clubs, normally open 1♣.

✓ Exercise discipline with your weak two-bids!

OPENING THE BIDDING

NOW TRY THESE...

Time for you to go to work. Fifteen hands follow. If you decide the hand is worth an opening bid, pick the bid you'd make. Answers and explanations follow – no peeking!

1   ♠ K J 5 2   ♥ A Q 4 2   ♦ 7 2   ♣ Q 7 3

2   ♠ A J 8 2   ♥ K 8 7 2   ♦ K   ♣ J 8 6 4

3   ♠ 7   ♥ A 8 7 5 2   ♦ K Q   ♣ Q 8 5 3 2

4   ♠ A 8 3   ♥ K J 8 7 2   ♦ K 6   ♣ K Q 4

5   ♠ K J 6 2   ♥ A J 8 2   ♦ 8 7 2   ♣ A 4

6   ♠ K J 10 8 7 2   ♥ Q 10 9 2   ♦ K 5   ♣ 6

7   ♠ A Q J 10 7 5   ♥ K J 6 2   ♦ 6 4   ♣ 3

8   ♠ A 6   ♥ A 3   ♦ K 8 4   ♣ 8 7 6 4 3 2

9   ♠ 6   ♥ K J 6 2   ♦ J 8 7 2   ♣ A K 6 2

10   ♠ J 8 7 5 2   ♥ K 4   ♦ A K J 7 2   ♣ 6

11   ♠ K J 4   ♥ 6   ♦ K 5 4 3   ♣ A 10 6 5 4

12   ♠ K 5   ♥ K 7 6 3   ♦ A 6   ♣ A Q 7 4 2

13   ♠ K Q 9 7 5   ♥ A Q 6   ♦ A K 5   ♣ K 5

14   ♠ A J 9 7 2   ♥ A 5   ♦ 7   ♣ K 9 7 5 3

15   ♠ A K J 5   ♥ 10 8 7 4 2   ♦ A 6   ♣ 9 2

ANSWERS

1	1♣	12 HCP, no 5-card major.
2	1♣	12 HCP, no 5-card major.
3	Pass	Only 11 HCP and the two 5-card suits aren't touching nor are they particularly good. A further negative feature is the 5 HCP tied up in the doubleton KQ.
4	1NT	16 HCP in a balanced hand. Don't worry about the 5-card major. It may be temporarily 'lost' but that isn't necessarily a bad thing and we may 'find' it again at a later stage of the auction.
5	1♦	The ugly one diamond — no 5-card major, no 3-card club suit but enough strength (13 HCP) to mandate opening.
6	Pass	The right HCP and good spade suit for a weak two-bid but the good quality hearts on the side should deter you from opening a weak two. Don't 'compromise' by opening a sub-par one-bid! There are hands that seem to have enough strength but don't fit the criteria for either a one-bid or a two-bid. Later developments in the auction will usually allow you the opportunity to bid these hands with greater accuracy if you haven't fudged on your opener.
7	1♠	Yes, only 11 HCP but a very good quality 6-card suit that will provide for easy rebids. Another positive feature is the side 4-card heart suit which will offer good prospects for game if we have a fit in either major. We would, however, also open 1♠ if the side 4-card suit was either diamonds or clubs.
8	Pass	Two distinct flaws – only 11 HCP and a truly awful long suit.
9	1♦	Enough strength (12 HCP) and diamonds instead of clubs for ease of rebid; remember, with 4-4 in the minors, open 1♦.
10	1♠	You have 12 HCP and you always open the higher of two 5-card suits regardless of relative quality (except with spades and clubs).
11	Pass	Only 11 HCP (1 flaw) and a poor longest suit (clubs). Also, we would have to consider opening 1♦ with this 4-5 minor shape and the diamonds are sub-par for this action.
12	1NT	An exception – just to see if you're paying attention – but the semi-balanced pattern and strong stoppers in the short suits make this a hand type best expressed with the notrump opening.
13	2NT	Also a notrump hand-type notwithstanding the 5-card major. 21 HCP, balanced, all suits stopped = a perfect description!
14	1♣	Minimum (12-15 HCP, sometimes 11 HCP) and very good (18+ HCP) black two-suiters are started with 1♣.
15	1♥	Enough HCP (12) to open and notwithstanding the relative weakness of the heart suit, it is our longest suit and does have five cards in it!

THE TWO-OVER-ONE
RESPONSE TO 1♥ or 1♠

♥ Tell your partner the glad news that you have a powerful hand at the earliest possible moment. *Criticus.* **Contract Simplicitas.** *1933.*

In Standard bidding, when partner opens one of a suit you are allowed to bid a new suit at the two-level with as few as 10 HCP. Over the years, several flaws have become evident in this approach:

- The low strength threshold for this action can get the partnership too high too quickly, without there being the fit or strength needed to take that many tricks.

- A great deal of the remaining available bidding space is taken up with distinguishing between hands where responder wants to invite to game and those where he wishes to force to game. As a result:

  a)   selecting the proper strain to play in often gets secondary attention

  b)   there is virtually no auction room left below game to explore slam possibilities.

BY THE WAY

The word 'strain' is used to mean 'suit or notrump' – when we talk about 'finding the right strain' it includes the possibility of playing in a trump contract or in notrump.

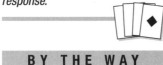

By adopting a much higher minimum strength requirement for responder to make a new suit bid at the two-level, Two-over-One tries to repair these shortcomings. There are only six possible auction starts that can include a simple two-level response to a one-level opening bid.

Opener Might Bid	Responder Might Bid
1♠	2♣ or 2♦ or 2♥
or	
1♥	2♣ or 2♦
or	
1♦	2♣

In this Step, I'm going to reduce the number of auctions we deal with to five – the five possible Two-over-One sequences that can occur after an opening bid of 1♥ or 1♠. (The 1♦-2♣ auction will be discussed in a later Step). I am going to add the further important proviso that responder must be an unpassed hand.

Critical Definition

Whenever responder has not passed previously and makes a simple two-level response in a new suit, the auction is 100% forcing to game. **No exceptions!**

If you don't think you are strong enough to insist on game opposite a possible minimum opener, don't make the Two-over-One response. What you might bid instead will be dealt with later, but remember that a two-level response in a new suit by an unpassed responder will get your side to game.

What do you need for the Two-over-One response?

The simplest answer to this question is to remember Equation #1 from your elementary bidding lessons:

$$O.B.+O.B.= G$$

An Opening Bid plus an Opening Bid equals a Game

In other words, to make a forcing-to-game two-level response in a new suit you must have the values for an opening bid. As we've seen in Step 2, this will usually mean 12+ HCP, but some exceptional 11 HCP hands will also qualify.

- ***Only a 4-card suit is required*** except for one specific sequence: for a 2♥ response to 1♠, you must have at least a 5-card suit.

- ***There is no effective upper limit*** for the Two-over-One response. As you will see in later Steps, we will be using Jump Shift responses for something other than the old-fashioned rock crusher hands. Accordingly, even if you hold

♠ A 7　♥ A Q J 10 7 2　♦ A K　♣ Q 7 2

a simple 2♥ response will be appropriate if your partner opens 1♠.

- **When you make a Two-over-One response in a new suit, you will frequently have 3-card support for opener's major;** indeed, this may be the only correct response with enough strength to force to game and 3-card support, but…

- **You will rarely have 4-card (or greater) support for opener's major** in a hand strong enough to force to game except when you have an excellent suit (usually 5+cards) of your own as a 'source of tricks'. So if partner opens 1♠ and you have

♠ K J 6 2　♥ 6 5　♦ Q 7　♣ A K Q 7 5

the correct response is 2♣ (the club suit is so strong it is a 'source of tricks') while with

♠ K J 6 2　♥ A 7　♦ K 7　♣ Q 8 7 3 2

a different response will be appropriate (the hand has 4-card support but the long suit is not an immediate 'source of tricks') — we'll see what that different response should be in the next Step.

If you are near a minimum to force to game (12-14 HCP) and your Two-over-One response would have to be in a very poor suit, you should avoid making the Two-over-One bid. When you make a Two-over-One response, your partner will expect that honors in your suit will be of more than ordinary value. You should avoid misleading him (just as you should not make an overcall on a bad suit even with a good hand). So with

♠ Q 7 3　♥ K Q 9 2　♦ A Q　♣ 8 7 3 2

opposite a 1♠ opening, you definitely have enough strength (13 HCP) to commit your side to game but a 2♥ response would promise at least five hearts and the club suit is so shabby as to be almost non-existent, thus ruling out a 2♣ response. You will be happy to know that after Step 5, you will be well equipped to deal with such problematic holdings.

BY THE WAY

'Source of tricks' is a very important concept that you'll be seeing lots more of in subsequent pages. An ace and a king and a queen may add up to 9 HCP but when you put them together in a 5-card suit, that 9 HCP may now be worth five tricks, far more than if that same 9 HCP were spread around three different suits (or if they were together but unaccompanied by any spot cards). One of the huge systemic gains afforded by the Two-over-One Approach is that you now have ways to show these 'sources of tricks' in the bidding.

Summary

- ✓ I recommend you play that a Two-over-One response to an opening bid by an unpassed hand is 100% forcing to game.

- ✓ In order to make a Two-over-One response, you must have at least an opening bid of your own, but your hand may also be extremely strong.

- ✓ A Two-over-One response promises at least a good quality 4-card suit, except for 2♥ over 1♠, which promises at least five hearts.

- ✓ A Two-over-One response may include 3-card support for partner's major.

- ✓ A Two-over-One response will only include 4-card support for partner's major if you have an exceptional source of tricks of your own that you wish to show.

THE TWO-OVER-ONE RESPONSE

NOW TRY THESE...

Based on what you've seen so far, would you make a Two-over-One response opposite the indicated opening bid holding the following hands?

♠ K J 6	**Partner Opens**	♠ 8 5	**Partner Opens**
♥ A Q 7 4	1) 1♠	♥ 7 2	3) 1♠
♦ 8 5	2) 1♥	♦ A Q J 8 7 3 2	4) 1♥
♣ K J 6 2		♣ J 5	
♠ K Q 6 4	**Partner Opens**	♠ 4	**Partner opens**
♥ A 6	5) 1♠	♥ A Q	7) 1♠
♦ 6 5	6) 1♥	♦ A 8 7 2	8) 1♥
♣ A K 10 6 4		♣ A K Q 8 7 4	
♠ 6	**Partner Opens**	♠ K 10 8	**Partner Opens**
♥ A Q 6 2	9) 1♠	♥ A J 6	11) 1♠
♦ K 7 6 5 2	10) 1♥	♦ K 5	12) 1♥
♣ A J 7		♣ Q 7 4 3 2	

♠ K Q 6 4   ***Partner Opens***   ♠ A Q 7 2   ***Partner Opens***
♥ 8 7   **13)** 1♠   ♥ 7   **15)** 1♠
♦ Q 5   **14)** 1♥   ♦ K Q 7 2   **16)** 1♥
♣ A 10 8 7 4   ♣ A Q 9 2

♠ 8   ***Partner Opens***   ♠ A 7   ***Partner Opens***
♥ 7   **17)** 1♠   ♥ Q J 7   **19)** 1♠
♦ K Q J 8 7   **18)** 1♥   ♦ K 10 8 2   **20)** 1♥
♣ A K J 8 7 2   ♣ A 10 7 2

ANSWERS

1 Yes 2♣   Game-going strength, reasonable clubs and only 3-card support for partner's suit.

2 No   4-card support and the clubs, while decent, are not the 5-card length a 'source of tricks' needs to be.

3 No   You do not have enough strength to bid 2♦ and thereby force to game.

4 No   See Problem 3.

5 Yes 2♣   More than enough strength to force to game and, with 4-card support, a good quality side suit as a 'source of tricks'.

6 Yes 2♣   Again, enough to insist on game and with clubs longer than spades, it is better to follow the natural course of bidding your longer suit first (see Problems 13 and 14 below).

7 Yes 2♣   You have a great hand and can make the natural and forcing-to-game response which will allow you to develop the auction and eventually make a decision about small slam/grand slam and possible strain. Remember, partner can't pass short of game once you've responded 2♣. Don't panic and don't be in a hurry!

8 Yes 2♣   See Problem 7.

9 Yes 2♦   Game-going strength and your natural bid.

10 No   Enough strength but with 4-card support, you need a 'source of tricks' side suit to make the Two-over-One (see Step 4).

11 Yes 2♣   Game-going strength and only 3-card support for partner's major. Remember, the quality control 'source of tricks' only applies in responding hands with 4-card support for partner's major.

12 Yes 2♣   See Problem 11.

13 No
Although you have great 4-card support and your side will likely get to game, you don't have the opening bid a 2♣ response would promise. What you should respond will be discussed in the next Step.

14 No
Your correct response is 1♠. You don't have enough strength to force to game by making the seemingly more natural bid of 2♣ so you can instead make the convenient 1-over-1 response that, as in Standard, promises only a minimum of 6 HCP and 4 cards in the suit bid. (Compare with problems 5 and 6 above).

15 No
You have 4-card support in a game-going hand without a source of tricks side suit, so you don't qualify for a Two-over-One (see Step 4).

16 No
Simply bid 1♠. Try always to go 'up the line' with 4-card suits. If you bid 2♣ just to establish a game-forcing auction and later bid spades, partner is entitled to expect a hand something like you had in Problem 3 above while if you don't ever bid spades, a 4-4 fit in that suit may go undiscovered.

17 Yes 2♣
Make your natural and forcing-to-game response and be grateful partner won't be passing below game as you try to ferret out your side's best fit.

18 Yes 2♣
See Problem 17.

19 Yes 2♣
Enough strength for game. In your formative stages as a bridge player, you might have responded 2NT with this type of hand to show 12-14 HCP in a balanced hand with the unbid suits stopped but we're going to use the 2NT response for something else (see the next Step).

20 Yes 2♣
Game-going strength and only 3-card support for partner.

BERGEN AND BEYOND

♥ There is nothing difficult in the appraisal of a supporting hand, yet many players seem to find it so. **The Official System of Contract Bridge.** *1931.*

Players who win at bridge are consistently successful at bidding games and, to a lesser extent, slams. The form of scoring — teams, pairs or rubber bridge — has very little bearing. Collect as many of those juicy game and/or slam bonuses as you possibly can and you will collect trophies, masterpoints and money — subject to availability, of course.

A little research will show that — notwithstanding the omnipresent 'Notrump Hogs' that turn up everywhere — more of those rewarding bonuses are collected for major-suit contracts than for either of the other two possible strains, notrump or minors. You can do some research — study the travelers at your next club game or check out the reports of World Championships — or take my word for it (I've done the research!) — the majors rule!

There are, of course, very good reasons for hearts and spades having such preeminence. With a good trump fit, you don't need as many HCP to underwrite a successful game contract in a major as you would in notrump. Nor do you need honor cards or stoppers in all suits — shortness in a suit the opponents are lusting to take tricks in will stop them in their tracks. And, of course, ten tricks will suffice for a major-suit game while eleven are needed in a minor, not to mention that you score more in a major.

It stands to reason, then, that any bidding system will do well if it increases the accuracy of finding major-suit fits and exploiting them to the maximum. The Standard bidding arsenal has several critical weaknesses in its approach to this, but they can be summarized as too-wide ranges in both strength (usually measured in HCP) and degree of fit (how many trumps does the supporter have?). Welcome to the world of Two-Over-One, with more narrowly defined and decidedly more accurate major-suit auctions.

The magical ninth trump

Before exhibiting all our weaponry, we need to introduce and get cozy with a concept that is startlingly simple but so fundamentally critical that it's totally amazing no bridge theorist came along to popularize it sooner.

Simply put, two combining hands with a nine-card fit will 'play better' and usually take more tricks than identically strong hands with only an eight-card fit. The difference — the 'ninth trump'! While expert players no doubt always realized this concept in a sort of unspoken, subliminal way, it wasn't until Marty Bergen and Larry Cohen (of 'The Law of Total Tricks' fame) emphasized the point in their writings, teachings and system design that it became part of popular bridge consciousness.

Let's look at a practical example. Suppose for a moment you're declarer in 4♠ on the following layout:

You	Dummy
♠ A Q J 4 2	♠ K 7 5
♥ Q 8 4	♥ 7 2
♦ 6	♦ A 8 7 2
♣ A 10 7 3	♣ K 8 4 2

This is a wonderful contract that, assuming reasonable breaks, suffers only from the one serious flaw that dooms so many otherwise promising contracts: it has to be played against opponents whose mission is to set you! A trump lead will not be good news. Since you can't make your game without disposing of a heart loser, you give up a heart trying to prepare for a ruff in the dummy. Back comes another trump, and inexorable fate overtakes you.

Now, make just one small change in the dummy:

You	Dummy
♠ A Q J 4 2	♠ K 7 6 5
♥ Q 8 4	♥ 7 2
♦ 6	♦ A 8 7
♣ A 10 7 3	♣ K 8 4 2

Regardless of the opponents' best efforts at denuding this dummy of its ruffing power, we will always be able eventually to ruff a heart loser in the dummy and make ten tricks.

Both our example dummies have the same HCP and side-suit distributional assets (the doubleton heart) but the ninth trump in the second dummy makes all the difference in the world. Let's take a look at a second example to illustrate the ninth trump's usefulness and how being aware of it can make you a better bidder. Suppose you hold:

♠ A K J 7 2   ♥ A 8 4 3   ♦ A 6 5 2   ♣ —

and you find out (how you do that will become apparent as we go along) that partner has 4-card spade support and at most a singleton heart. Now you know that you effectively have no heart losers, regardless of the defenders' machinations, as you can plan to ruff all three losers in dummy using the ♦A and a club ruff as entries to your hand — the plan being made before you ever see dummy! Naturally, if dummy had only three spades, the ruff-all-the-heart-losers plan might be derailed by a trump lead. One more winner, one fewer loser — if the ninth trump is present.

Since we're working on a basis of promising five cards in the suit for an opening bid of 1♥ or 1♠, we can increase our accuracy in game and/or slam bidding by focusing on these two crucial goals:

1. Narrowing the HCP ranges for most raises, and

2. Separating hands which have 3-card trump support from those with 4-card support, when that ever-so-useful ninth trump will be present.

In order to do this, we're going to use some direct raises that will get us up to the three-level — but fear not. Another offshoot of the Ninth Trump theory and the Law of Total Tricks is the idea that you will be safe at the three-level when you have that ninth trump — which means any time you have four cards in support opposite a 5-card major opening.

Let's look at the various ways we can raise partner's major directly.

The constructive single raise

Partner	You	Partner	You
1♠	2♠	1♥	2♥

When you (as an unpassed hand responder) raise your partner's major opening one level, it is a constructive single raise. You will have 7-10 HCP and exactly three cards in support — never more than three.

Here are three examples of a constructive single raise of 1♠ to 2♠:

♠ Q 7 5	♠ Q 6 4	♠ A 10 5
♥ A Q 6 2	♥ K 8 7 3	♥ K 7 5 2
♦ 6 2	♦ Q J 7 2	♦ 8
♣ 8 7 4 3	♣ Q 6	♣ 10 7 6 5 2
8 HCP	*10 HCP but 'poor' — queens and jacks.*	*7 HCP — but 'good'*

Here are three hands with which you should not make a constructive single raise:

♠ Q 8 7	♠ K 8 5	♠ K Q 8 2
♥ Q 8 6 2	♥ A 9	♥ A 8
♦ Q 10 5	♦ K 10 7 6 5	♦ 9 8 4 3
♣ J 8 6	♣ 8 7 2	♣ 9 6 3
The 7 HCP are very 'poor' value.	*Two kings and an ace make this 10 HCP 'good' — too good!*	*9 HCP but 4 trumps — too many!*

Bergen raises

Now we come to our direct raises with 4-card trump support. Remember, there will be safety at the three-level with a combined holding of nine (or more) trumps, so using a three-level response to show four trumps is not hazardous. At the same time, since in sequences like 1♠-2♣ the responder has no upper limit to his strength, you don't need to jump shift to show great power opposite an opening bid. The jump shifts to 3♣ and 3♦ can be used instead to show 4-card raises — known as Bergen Raises to recognize Marty Bergen, the original formulator of the idea.

These are the Bergen meanings for 3♣ and 3♦ responses to an opening bid of 1♥ or 1♠:

Partner	You
1♥ *or* 1♠	3♦

An old-fashioned limit raise with 10-12 HCP and four trumps (rarely five, but never three). A typical hand over a 1♠ opening would be

♠ A J 7 2   ♥ A 3   ♦ Q 6 5 2   ♣ 7 6 3

Partner	You
1♥ *or* 1♠	3♣

A 4-card constructive raise: 7-10 HCP and four trumps (rarely five, but never three). A typical hand over a 1♠ opening would be

♠ A J 7 2   ♥ 6 3   ♦ Q 6 5 2   ♣ 7 6 3

Preemptive raises

Everyone recognizes that you should try to take away the opponents' bidding space if the deal 'belongs' to them — that's why calls like weak two-bids or preemptive three-level openings are popular. When partner opens the bidding in a major, you can use the power of that ninth trump when responder is weak defensively to harass the opponents as much as possible.

Partner	You		Partner	You
1♠	3♠		1♥	3♥

These immediate double raises are preemptive: no more than 6 HCP, always four trumps (on occasion five, especially for those of you who are a little gunshy at first about bidding so high with so little!). Here are some examples of hands on which you could use this bid if partner opened 1♠:

♠ Q 8 7 3	♠ J 8 6 5 3	♠ K 9 8 5
♥ 8 7	♥ 6	♥ Q 9 8 7 4
♦ Q 8 5 3	♦ 9 6 5	♦ 8 3
♣ 10 7 5	♣ 8 6 5 4	♣ 5 2

Life in the fast lane, eh? Sure, it's a little scary, but all kinds of things might happen subsequently. Here are some of them:

- Your partner might get left there and make the contract (hooray!) or go down and, if the latter, you're hoping the amount he goes down is less than the opponents might have scored left to their own devices (it usually is).

- The opponents might get too high, or stay too low or get to the wrong strain — all things which the pressure of the auction frequently causes to happen.

- The opponents might still bid and get to their best con-tract (rats!) but look at all the fun you'll have had bid-ding with nothing. Nothing ventured, nothing gained.

- They might double you and try for a penalty to teach you a sharp lesson for your impertinence. This happens very rarely but at least partner will be declaring these possible disasters.

Direct game raise

Partner	You		Partner	You
1♠	4♠		1♥	4♥

Much the same as in classic Standard, we will raise one of a major directly to game with fewer than 10 HCP, 5-card trump support (sometimes more!) and some distributional help (a singleton or perhaps two doubletons) on the side. Since the auction is now in the stratosphere, the opponents are less likely to bid and most of the time four of the major will be the final contract — beware! Here are two example hands for a bid of 4♠ in response to partner's 1♠ opening bid:

♠ A 8 7 6 2
♥ 7
♦ K 9 7 6
♣ 9 5 4

A classic: five trumps, less than 10 HCP, some distributional assets

♠ A Q 9 8 6
♥ 7 2
♦ 8 2
♣ J 8 5 4

Less than 10 HCP, five trumps, some distributional assets

But note that with something like

♠ K 7 4 3 2 ♥ 6 3 ♦ 6 5 2 ♣ 7 6 3

you should be content to raise only to 3♠. Even though you have five trumps, your hand is too flat to risk a jump to the four-level.

A conventional game raise — Jacoby 2NT

Believe it or not, sometimes you'll hold a really good hand with game-going strength and four (or more) cards in partner's major. With this hand we are going to use 2NT as an *artificial game-forcing raise of partner's major*. This conventional bid is called the **Jacoby Two Notrump**. (Yes, the same family that brought you those ubiquitous transfers — but that's a story for another day!)

By definition, the 2NT response by an unpassed hand shows a hand with:

- *4-card support (occasionally five trumps, but absolutely never only three)*
- *12 + HCP*
- *no singleton or void in a side suit, except occasionally a singleton ace*
- *no great side suit that could be an independent 'source of tricks', for example AKQ105*

As we'll see, lots of fun things can happen after this response but two things are 100% guaranteed:

1. We are going at least to game.
2. Partner's major suit will be trumps.

These hands are good examples of a 2NT response to 1♠ opening bid:

♠ A Q 7 5	♠ K J 7 3 2	♠ K 9 7 6
♥ K J 5 3	♥ A 6 2	♥ A
♦ 8 2	♦ K J 5	♦ K Q 4 2
♣ A 5 2	♣ Q 4	♣ K J 7 2

but you should avoid making a Jacoby 2NT response to 1♠ with these hands:

♠ K Q J ♥ A 4 ♦ K 8 7 5 ♣ A 9 3 2

Lots of HCP (17) but only 3-card support. Respond 2♣, natural and game-forcing instead.

♠ K 8 7 5 ♥ 8 2 ♦ 9 3 ♣ A K Q J 5

Yes, 4-card support and game-going strength but you also have a 'source of tricks' on the side. Respond 2♣ instead.

♠ A Q 6 2 ♥ A 8 7 2 ♦ K 8 7 4 ♣ 6

Again, 4-card support and game-going values but this time with a side-suit singleton which you're going to see how to show in the next section.

Splinter bids

Once a fit has been established and you know you are going to game, it can be very useful for evaluating slam prospects to know how well the two hands 'fit'. Suppose for a moment you've opened 1♠ with

♠ K J 10 9 5 ♥ K 6 ♦ A Q ♣ 8 7 5 3

and partner has the hand I just showed in the previous section:

♠ A Q 6 2 ♥ A 8 7 2 ♦ K 8 7 4 ♣ 6

A small slam in spades will be made rather easily simply by ruffing at least two club losers in the dummy and discarding the third club (if necessary) on a diamond winner. After a one-of-a-major opening bid, you can use a Splinter Bid to show a hand like this one in response.

There are basically only six possible auctions after the major opening that are immediately defined as Splinter Bids:

Opener	Responder
1♥	3♠ or 4♣ or 4♦
1♠	4♣ or 4♦ or 4♥

Using these bids to mean you hold a lot of the suit named is wasteful of bidding space and isn't going to be needed very often, so it is more productive to use them to mean:

- *at least 12 HCP*
- *at least 4-card support for partner's major (sometimes five but never three)*
- *a singleton or void in the bid suit (but not a singleton ace)*

These splinter raises are forcing to game (of course — you're already that high!) and slam-invitational, subject to discovering the right 'fit' and 'controls' — more about that later.

Yes, but...

If you've been paying very careful attention, you'll have noticed I've created some gaps. Yes, there are some hands with support for partner's major-suit opening that you can't yet describe — for example, a 10-12 HCP hand with 3-card support or a 6 HCP hand with 3-card support. Unlike over- or under-sized fish, you can't just throw these hands back, but you will know how to bid them after the next Step.

Summary

After an opening bid of one of a major, an unpassed hand responder has the following direct raises available:

✓ 2 Major = 7-10 HCP, 3-card support (Constructive Single Raise).

✓ 3 Major = less than 7 HCP, 4- or 5-card support (Preemptive Raise).

✓ 4 Major = less than 10 HCP, at least 5-card support, some distributional help, usually a side-suit singleton or void or two doubletons.

✓ 3♦ = 10-12 HCP, 4-card support (Limit Raise — Bergen).

✓ 3♣ = 7-10 HCP, 4-card support (4-card Constructive Raise — Bergen).

✓ 2NT = Jacoby Game-Forcing Raise, at least 4-card support, 12+HCP, no singleton or void on the side, no 'source of tricks'.

✓ Double jumps in a new suit = Splinter Bids showing a singleton or void in the suit bid, with at least 4-card support and 12+HCP.

DIRECT MAJOR-SUIT RAISES

NOW TRY THESE...

Your partner has opened 1♠ as dealer. What is your response on each of the following hands?

1	♠ K 8 7	2	♠ A 8 7 6 5	3	♠ K J 6 4	4	♠ K J 4 2
	♥ A Q 8 2		♥ 7		♥ 8 3		♥ 9 2
	♦ 10 7 6 5		♦ J 8 7 6 4		♦ Q 3		♦ A 7 2
	♣ 10 3		♣ 9 2		♣ A K Q 10 5		♣ K Q 9 2

5	♠ K J 7 3	6	♠ 7 6 5 2	7	♠ J 8 7 2	8	♠ A 8 7 6 4
	♥ A J 9 2		♥ A 4		♥ 8		♥ 8
	♦ 8 7 2		♦ K 4		♦ 8 7 4 2		♦ A Q 4
	♣ 9 2		♣ A 8 7 5 2		♣ 10 8 7 4		♣ K 8 7 2

ANSWERS

1 2♠ A classic 3-card constructive raise.

2 4♠ Less than 10 HCP, 5 trumps and some distributional help.

3 2♣ Game-going values plus 4-card support and a very real 'source of tricks'. You might survive in the bidding if you chose 2NT as a Jacoby forcing raise instead but you will soon see how valuable it can be to start with 2♣.

4 2NT This is the right type of hand for the Jacoby forcing raise — 13 HCP, 4-card support plus no 'source of tricks' and no singleton (or void) on the side.

5 3♣ A 4-card Constructive Raise with 4 trumps and 9 HCP. Perfect!

6 3♦ A 4-card Limit Raise with 11 HCP.

7 3♠ Fun, wow! Preemptive Raises at their finest!

8 4♥ A splinter bid promising at least 4-card support, game-going strength and a singleton or void in hearts. Hope partner is awake!

THE FORCING
1NT RESPONSE

> ♥ Someone, it would seem, has told them that the bidding of such a hand is difficult, and they have believed it. **The Official System of Contract Bridge.** *1931.*

You will already have realized that by reserving our Two-over-One responses to an opening bid for game-forcing hands, we have created a new problem. We need some way to distinguish all those 10-12 HCP hands from the minimum response 6-9 HCP hands. In Two-over-One, we use a common feature of most modern systems that are based on five-card major-suit openings: the Forcing Notrump.

As you'll remember from your Standard background, the classic 1NT response to a one-of-a-major opening shows 6-9 HCP, denies support for opener's major, usually denies being at the upper end of the range with a long (6+ cards) suit, and can be passed. In Two-over-One, if you have not previously passed, your response of 1NT to a 1♥ or 1♠ opening is forcing for one round – opener may not pass. In addition to the systemic advantages you'll soon see, you may well find it a relief not to have to play hopeless 1NT contracts because you made a Standard 1NT response and partner had nothing more to say! For the Forcing 1NT response, your strength will range from 5-12 HCP. There are even some rare hands in the 13-14 HCP range with which you'll want to respond 1NT!

Of course, if you can bid your own suit at the one-level, you still do so, just as you did playing Standard. On this hand

♠ A 6 3 2   ♥ 7 6   ♦ K 9 7 5   ♣ 8 7 3

you would still bid 1♠ if partner opened 1♥. However, the Forcing 1NT response is made on all other hands that warrant a response but that aren't strong enough to make an immediate force to game (when a Two-over-One response would be used). In addition, some hands that have support for partner's major but that don't fit into our scheme of ways to raise partner immediately will start with a Forcing 1NT response.

Typical Forcing 1NT responses to a 1♠ opening

Partner	You
1♠	1NT

Let's look at the various types of hand on which you are going to use the Forcing Notrump. For convenience, we'll assume partner has opened 1♠, but the same principles apply after a 1♥ opening. Don't worry for now about how the auction continues, although we will indicate some of the possibilities below; we'll cover them in much more detail in Step 9.

1) Nondescript hands with enough points to respond in general.

♠ 7 6	♠ K 8	♠ 5 2	♠ 10 4
♥ K J 3	♥ 8 7 4 2	♥ Q 5 2	♥ K Q 8 2
♦ Q 9 8 2	♦ A 9 7 6 4	♦ K Q J 8 2	♦ 10 7 6 5
♣ 9 6 4 2	♣ 6 2	♣ J 6 2	♣ 8 7 4

On these hands, you're probably going to pass partner's rebid – but more on that in Step 9.

2) Hands with 5-7 HCP with either 3- or 4-card support for spades that are either too good (usually because of an outside ace) for an immediate pre-emptive double raise (1♠-3♠) or not quite good enough for an immediate 3-card constructive raise (1♠-2♠) or 4-card constructive raise (1♠-3♣).

♠ Q 8 3	♠ 8 7 4 2	♠ K Q 4
♥ K J 6 2	♥ 10 9	♥ 10 9 8 7
♦ 8 7 6	♦ A J 7 6	♦ Q 6 4
♣ 10 9 4	♣ J 6 5	♣ 5 4 2

On all these hands, I would start with 1NT and later support spades. If partner rebids 2♠, the plan is to pass.

3) *Hands with 10-12 HCP and precisely 3-card support for partner's major* – too weak for an immediate forcing-to-game Two-over-One response; the right strength but not enough support (at least four cards needed) for an immediate limit raise (3♦).

♠ K J 5	♠ A 10 5	♠ 7 6 5
♥ A 9 8 7 2	♥ 6	♥ K J 4
♦ Q J 4 2	♦ K Q J 7 5	♦ A Q 4 2
♣ 7	♣ 5 4 3 2	♣ J 7 6

On these hands, start with 1NT and then jump raise spades. If partner rebids 2♠, you will raise to 3♠.

4) *Weak unbalanced hands with a long suit or suits.*

♠ 6	♠ 7 4	♠ 4 3
♥ K J 8 7 6 2	♥ 4	♥ K 4
♦ Q 4 3 2	♦ J 9 7 6 5 4	♦ 10 2
♣ 7 2	♣ A Q 3 2	♣ A J 7 6 5 4 2

You will start with 1NT, and then bid your own best suit at the two-level over partner's rebid. If you can't do that (say partner rebids his spade suit), you will pass.

5) *Balanced or unbalanced hands that are strong enough to invite game* but not force to game, usually in the 10-12 HCP range.

♠ Q 4	♠ 7	♠ 7 6
♥ K J 3	♥ A 5 4 3	♥ 6
♦ K J 4 3	♦ K 8 7 6	♦ A 10 6 5 4
♣ Q 4 3 2	♣ A 10 7 4	♣ K Q J 6 2

Start with 1NT and then, with a balanced hand like the first example, bid 2NT over partner's rebid. With the other two hands, you will have to choose between bidding one of your suits at the three-level, raising spades (of course, partner will expect three of them) or trying 2NT anyway.

6) *Exceptional Hands.* As you'll find with experience with Two-over-One, you won't like making a game-forcing natural response on a poor suit even though you may have enough high-card strength to do so, since partner will usually count on some offensive trick-taking potential in the suit you respond in. Also, the auction 1♠-2♥ promises at least a 5-card heart suit. This will sometimes lead you to a response of 1NT (as the 'least of evils') to partner's 1♠ with a hand like

♠ J 4 ♥ A K Q 4 ♦ A 3 2 ♣ 6 5 4 2

Usually, nothing bad will happen since partner is forced to rebid and you'll get another chance to show extra strength.

BY THE WAY

The Forcing 1NT response can often be thought of as a NOT bid – the hand's NOT right for anything else so bid 1NT! One of the most useful functions of the Forcing 1NT is that you start by telling partner, 'My hand is NOT this and NOT that' and, since partner is forced to rebid and give you a second chance, you'll soon be able to describe what it actually is.

Summary

✓ A 1NT response to 1♥ or 1♠ by an unpassed hand promises 5-12 HCP and is absolutely forcing for 1 round – opener must find a rebid!

✓ Without support for opener's major, you may be either unbalanced or balanced and are simply showing enough strength for a response but not enough to force to game.

✓ You also respond 1NT on some hands with support for opener's major: those with 5-7 HCP and 3- or 4-card support and those with 10-12 HCP and precisely 3-card support.

✓ Remember: since opener must rebid, you are going to get a second chance to complete the description of your hand.

THE FORCING 1NT

NOW TRY THESE...

What is your next bid on each of the following hands?

1   ♠ 3
    ♥ K J 5
    ♦ 9 8 7 6 3
    ♣ Q 7 6 2

Partner	You
1♥	?

2   ♠ 9 2
    ♥ 5
    ♦ 8 6 3
    ♣ A Q J 7 6 4 2

Partner	You
1♥	?

3   ♠ A J 7
    ♥ Q 3
    ♦ K 10 6 2
    ♣ J 10 6 2

Partner	You
1♥	?

4   ♠ 5 2
    ♥ 6
    ♦ A J 8 4 2
    ♣ K Q 8 4 2

Partner	You
1♥	?

5   ♠ K J 5
    ♥ 8 6 3
    ♦ A 8 7 2
    ♣ J 10 9

Partner	You
1♥	?

6   ♠ 6
    ♥ Q 7 5 2
    ♦ A 10 6 2
    ♣ 9 6 5 4

Partner	You
1♥	?

7   ♠ A K 7 2
    ♥ 7 2
    ♦ 8 7 4 2
    ♣ 10 6 5

Partner	You
1♥	?

8   ♠ K 10 3
    ♥ J 3
    ♦ K J 6 2
    ♣ K J 5 2

Partner	You
1♥	?

9   ♠ A 6
    ♥ K 10 6
    ♦ A 9 7 5 3
    ♣ 8 7 3

Partner	You
1♥	?

10 ♠ A Q
    ♥ 9 3
    ♦ A K J 4
    ♣ 10 8 7 5 2

Partner	You
1♥	?

ANSWERS

1   **1NT**   Not strong enough for a Two-over-One game force of 2♦ and the wrong combination of trumps and strength for any immediate heart raise. 1NT by default, planning to pass a 2♥ rebid, and to bid 2♥ yourself if partner rebids 2♣ or 2♦.

2   **1NT**   Not enough strength for a game-forcing Two-over-One response of 2♣ but certainly enough strength for a response. What you do next, if anything, will depend on what you hear from partner (see Step 9).

3   **1NT**   11 HCP – certainly enough strength for a bid or two but not enough for a game-forcing response of 2♣ so 1NT by default. You will likely bid 2NT next time round.

4   **1NT**   Unbalanced but not enough strength for a Two-over-One game-forcing response in a minor. Again, what you do next, if anything, will depend on what you hear from partner (see Step 9).

5   **2♥**   A constructive single raise promising 3 trumps and 8-10 HCP. Even with a flat hand like this one, you are too good to bid 1NT first and then 2♥ (5-7).

6   **1NT**   This is a toughie! You're too good for a preemptive raise to 3♥ and not quite good enough for an immediate constructive raise (3♦) which promises about 7-10 HCP with 4 trumps. With more experience playing the system, you might decide that the fourth trump will atone for some of the missing strength and respond 2♥ anyway — a sort of compromise based on the extra trump, as well as an ace and a ruffing value.

7   **1♠**   This one, however, is easy! In this quiz, as in real life at the table, not all bids are difficult to find!

8   **1NT**   On the borderline of having enough for the game-forcing response of 2♣ but the hand consists mostly of 'junky' points. With all those K-J combinations, there is also some theoretical value in having the opening lead in a notrump contract coming towards, rather than through, your hand. You will probably bid 2NT next time around to show your strength.

9   **1NT**   Nothing else fits. You don't have enough strength for an immediate game-forcing response of 2♦ and you are a trump short for an immediate limit raise of 3♣ (which would otherwise be right on strength).

10   **2♣**   More than enough strength for a natural Two-over-One game-forcing response even though your longest suit isn't as good as you might like. It's worth noting that you might survive with a 1NT response as you will get another turn to bid, but a hand this good will be hard to describe, as you'll see in later Steps.

OTHER RESPONSES
TO 1♥ OR 1♠

> ♥ I divide bids into tentative bids and attacking bids. *Criticus.*
> **Contract Simplicitas.** *1933.*

The language of bridge bidding has a very limited vocabulary:

- *The numbers 1 through 7 inclusive*
- *Spades, hearts, diamonds, clubs and notrump*
- *Pass*
- *Double*
- *Redouble*

Not a lot to work with when you consider that there are 53,644,737,765,488,792,839,237,440,000 possible deals to describe! Worse still, the rules of bridge grammar are such that as the auction progresses there are fewer words available to us, while some of the words can only be used if our opponents give us the opportunity.

Since the vocabulary and syntax are both limited, we don't want to waste any opportunities to mold them to our purpose. What you may find hard to believe is that, after taking a mere five Steps so far, we have just about exhausted all possible responses to an opening bid of 1♥ or 1♠. This Step will be concerned with useful meanings for the remaining four possible sequences. The first is by far the most important.

1) *The 1♠ response to 1♥.*

Partner	You
1♥	1♠

In many respects this is the easiest response as you are simply promising at least four spades and 6+ HCP. But many players selfishly go out of their way to bid their own spades in this situation when they would be better advised to raise their partner's hearts immediately. In general, hands that fit one of the ways we've seen to raise partner's major immediately should do so, notwithstanding the fact that they may also contain four or more spades. Break the good news to partner: 'We have a fit!'

Here are some examples of what to do when partner opens 1♥:

♠ A Q 6 5 3   ♥ Q 8 7   ♦ 8 2   ♣ 10 7 6

Raise 1♥ to 2♥ — a 3-card constructive raise with 8-10 HCP.

♠ A Q 4 2   ♥ K J 10 3   ♦ 5 3   ♣ 8 7 2

Respond 3♦ — a 4 card limit raise with 10-12 HCP.

♠ K J 7 6 5   ♥ A J 8 7   ♦ 6 3   ♣ 9 2

Respond 3♣ — 4-card constructive raise with 8-10 HCP. But with

♠ A Q 4 2   ♥ K Q 6   ♦ 7 6 5 4   ♣ 9 3

respond 1♠, natural and forcing one round, as no immediate raise of hearts with 3-card support and 10-12 HCP is available. Note that this is a parallel situation to

♠ 10 8   ♥ K Q 6   ♦ A Q 4 2   ♣ 8 5 3 2

with which you had to respond 1NT, also forcing one round, since no immediate heart raise was available and you weren't strong enough for a game-forcing Two-over-One response.

2) *The jump to 2♠ over 1♥.*

Partner	You
1♥	2♠

I like to use this response as a weak jump shift (WJS). (As you will see in a later Step, I will also recommend using the WJS over minor-suit openings.) For this bid you should have:

- a 6-card suit (rarely 7)
- 3-7 HCP
- no more than two hearts

In other words, you will have a weak hand with long spades and no heart support – possibly even worse than the worst hand that you might open a weak two-bid on.

BY THE WAY

This use for 1♥-2♠, along with the remaining ideas in this section, is strictly optional. If you decide not to bother with it, you won't harm anything. You can ignore it completely, or add it later if you wish. You just won't have a meaning for these specific sequences, but that's not the end of the world. Not everything has to mean something!

For example

♠ K 10 9 5 4 3 ♥ 6 ♦ 8 7 6 ♣ 4 3 2

is an acceptable minimum 2♠ response to 1♥, especially not vulnerable.

♠ A Q 7 6 5 3 ♥ 7 6 ♦ 4 3 2 ♣ 5 2

This, in contrast, is a good WJS response of 2♠ over partner's 1♥.

3) *The 3♥ response to 1♠.*

Partner	You
1♠	3♥

Every system has its problem hands, and Two-over-One is no exception. Invitational strength (9-11 HCP) hands with six or seven hearts can be difficult to handle over a 1♠ opening bid, so I recommend that you use the direct 3♥ response to show this. You should not have more than two spades for this response. You might have either of these hands:

♠ 3 ♥ A Q J 9 6 5 ♦ K 4 3 ♣ 5 4 3

♠ 6 ♥ K J 10 6 5 4 3 ♦ A 7 4 ♣ 6 4

You won't use this bid very often, but it will be very useful when it does come up.

4) *The 3NT response to 1♥ or 1♠.*

Partner	You
1♥ *or* 1♠	3NT

As a very bulky, space-consuming bid, the immediate response of 3NT goes a bit against the grain of the Two-over-One philosophy of bidding slowly with good hands and using up auction space fast when you are weak, especially when you have a known fit. However, if you maintain some rigid standards, this 3NT response can be useful. I recommend that you use the 3NT response to show 15-17 HCP with specifically 3-3-3-4 or 3-3-4-3 shape and stoppers in all unbid suits. With that agreement,

♠ A 5 4 ♥ Q J 6 ♦ K J 10 3 ♣ A J 3

would be a perfect 3NT response over either 1♥ or 1♠.

Summary

UNPASSED HAND RESPONSES

	1♥ OPENING	1♠ OPENING
1♠	4+ spades; 6+HCP/forcing 1 rd	not available
1NT	5-12 HCP (rarely more) forcing 1 round	same
2♣/2♦	natural, opening bid+ forcing to game	same
2♥	constructive raise 8-10 HCP; 3-card support	natural, opening bid+ forcing to game; 5+ hearts
2♠	Weak Jump Shift 3-7 HCP, two or fewer hearts 6 (rarely 7) spades	constructive raise 8-10 HCP 3-card support
2NT	Jacoby Game Forcing Raise 4+ trumps Opening Bid+ Usually no singleton or void No side-suit source of tricks	same
3♣	constructive raise; 7-10 HCP 4-card support (occasionally 5)	same
3♦	limit raise; 10-12 HCP 4-card support (occasionally 5)	same
3♥	preemptive raise; 0-6 HCP 4-card support (occasionally 5)	natural and invitational 9-11 HCP; 6- or 7-card suit
3♠	splinter raise of hearts singleton or void in spades at least 4-card support 12+HCP; game-forcing	preemptive raise 0-6 HCP, 4-card support (occasionally 5)
3NT	natural; 15-17 HCP 3-3-3-4 or 3-3-4-3 shape unbid suits stopped	same
4♣/4♦	splinter raise	same
4♥	direct game raise 5+ hearts less than 10 HCP	splinter raise
4♠	to play!	direct game raise 5+spades less than 10 HCP

RESPONSES TO MAJOR-SUIT OPENINGS

NOW TRY THESE...

Partner opens 1♥ — what is your response?

1
- ♠ K J 10 6
- ♥ 10 6 2
- ♦ A 6 4 2
- ♣ 8 5

2
- ♠ A 6 4 3 2
- ♥ K 7 5 3 2
- ♦ 6 2
- ♣ 4

3
- ♠ A 10 6 5 3 2
- ♥ 6
- ♦ J 6 4
- ♣ 7 5 2

4
- ♠ K J 4
- ♥ Q 6 2
- ♦ K Q J
- ♣ A 10 7 2

5
- ♠ K 10 6 2
- ♥ A J 4
- ♦ K 8 4 2
- ♣ 6 3

Partner opens 1♠ — what is your response?

6
- ♠ K J 2
- ♥ A Q J 6 2
- ♦ A 4
- ♣ Q 10 4

7
- ♠ Q 10 6 2
- ♥ A Q 8 4
- ♦ Q J 4
- ♣ 6 2

8
- ♠ K 8 5 2
- ♥ 6
- ♦ Q 10 6 2
- ♣ 8 7 5 2

9
- ♠ K J 4
- ♥ Q 6 2
- ♦ K Q J
- ♣ A 10 6 2

10
- ♠ 6 4
- ♥ A Q J 9 6 2
- ♦ K 10 4
- ♣ 6 5

ANSWERS

1 2♥ 8-10 HCP, 3-card constructive raise. Don't get sidetracked by bidding spades — you'll lose the chance to tell partner about the exact nature of your fit for his major.

2 4♥ Again, you have a fit — make the direct game raise that describes your hand very well — less than 10 HCP, 5-card support, distributional help. Perfect!

3 2♠ A classic example of a Weak Jump Shift.

4 3NT 15-17 HCP, balanced, unbid suits stopped.

5 1♠ No direct heart raise describes this hand so you start with your spade suit and, if possible, make a jump preference later to show a 3-card limit raise. Remember, this is the hand type you would have to start with 1NT Forcing if you didn't have four spades.

6 2♥ Natural Two-over-One game force with spades to tell about later.

7 3♦ 10-12 HCP and 4-card support for partner.

8 3♠ A tidy little example of a preemptive raise.

9 2♣ This may look familiar (see 4 above). If you think it's the same you might respond 3NT but you really don't have all the unbid suits stopped so you might be better advised to reply 2♣ and support partner's spades at your next turn. Even a great player like you doesn't have to declare notrump on every deal!

10 3♥ Natural, 6+ cards and game-invitational, a specialized response that suits this collection very well.

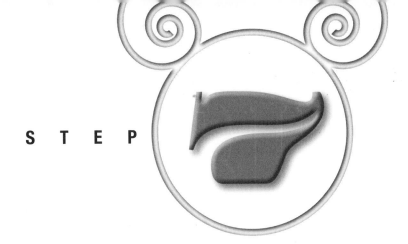

S T E P

AFTER A TWO-OVER-ONE RESPONSE

Well, you've finally opened the bidding and got past the first response. Now, let's get on to some serious bidding!

In natural bidding methods, constructive bidding is geared towards the accurate selection both of the **level** the partnership is going to play at — partscore, game or slam — and the **strain** the contract will be played in — major, minor or notrump. In Standard methods, after an unpassed hand makes a two-level response in a new suit, none of those level or strain issues have been resolved.

After a Two-over-One response, we have at least ruled out partscores from the level equation. This creates a lot of bidding options in the auctions we can have below game since both partners know that they will not stop bidding before (at least) game has been reached. In brief, we will devote the below-game space to an accurate search for the proper strain; we will also very often be able to explore slam possibilities on the way to game.

After the game-forcing Two-over-One response by an unpassed hand, opener's possible rebids will go a long way towards telling responder where and/or how high the partnership is heading. Let's look at what they are and what they promise.

Rebidding 2NT

You	Partner
1♠	2♣
2NT	

This simple notrump rebid will usually show 12-14 HCP in a balanced hand with the unbid suits stopped. On occasion, you may instead have 18-19 HCP in a balanced hand with the unbid suits stopped. (What about 15-17 HCP, balanced? Well, if you don't know the answer to that one, maybe you skipped over the introduction…) Don't worry if you have the stronger hand — partner will bid assuming you have the 12-14 HCP variety and you will get another chance to show your extra strength.

So, after 1♠ – 2♣, rebid 2NT with any of these hands:

♠ Q 10 6 5 2　♥ A 10 5　♦ K J 7　♣ Q 4

♠ A J 8 7 3　♥ Q J 6　♦ A Q 4　♣ 7 2

♠ K Q J 7 6　♥ A Q 4　♦ K Q 8　♣ Q 8

Rebidding a new suit without reversing

Stop the presses! Before you know that you're not reversing, you need to know what a reverse is. Simply put, a reverse by opener is a simple bid in a new suit that is higher than the cheapest possible rebid of his first suit. As you'll see, this rebid promises extra values beyond a simple minimum opener but for now just remember that:

You	Partner
1♥	2♣
2♠	

is a reverse because it is a simple (non-jump, remember) bid of spades and is higher than 2♥, the cheapest possible rebid of hearts. Similarly

You	Partner
1♠	2♦
3♣	

is also a reverse because, while it is a simple bid of clubs, it is higher than 2♠, the cheapest available rebid of spades.

With that out of the way, we can now summarize by saying that the simple non-reverse bid of a new suit merely promises 4+ cards in the bid suit without putting any effective limits on the upper end of the strength shown.

So, after

You	Partner
1♠	2♣
?	

you would rebid 2♥ with any of these hands:

♠ A Q 8 7 5 ♥ Q 4 3 2 ♦ K Q 2 ♣ 6

♠ A Q 9 7 5 ♥ K Q 6 5 2 ♦ Q 8 ♣ 9

♠ A K J 4 2 ♥ K Q J 7 ♦ A J 7 ♣ 6

Reversing

Now that I've defined a reverse, let's talk about what it shows. A reverse promises extra values beyond a minimum opener (usually 16+ HCP to be considered extra); also, the second suit bid is always shorter than the first. So, after

You	Partner
1♥	2♦
?	

you can rebid 2♠ with:

♠ K Q 4 2 ♥ A Q J 7 3 ♦ A 4 ♣ 6 2

(16 HCP, longer hearts than spades), but not with

♠ A Q 4 2 ♥ K J 7 6 5 ♦ Q 3 ♣ 7 5

where you have only 12 HCP or with

♠ A Q 8 7 6 ♥ K Q J 6 5 ♦ A 5 ♣ 4

where you have enough strength for a reverse but should have opened 1♠ in the first place. Don't forsake the natural order of bidding your suits just to impress the world with your knowledge of reverses. Similarly, after

You	Partner
1♠	2♥
?	

you can rebid 3♦ with

♠ A Q 8 7 2 ♥ 7 ♦ K Q J 8 ♣ K Q 6

since you have 17 HCP and longer spades than diamonds, but not with

♠ A Q 7 6 5 ♥ 6 ♦ K Q J 6 ♣ 6 5 4

where you have only 12 HCP, not enough for a reverse.

BY THE WAY

The matter of reverses is an area of some controversy among expert users of Two-over-One bidding. One school of thought likes to maintain the extra-strength parameters I have discussed so far but there is an opposing view with many adherents. This camp says that, since the bidding is already forcing to game, the opener should be allowed to show his shape without regard to minimum or extra values. There are pluses and minuses to both approaches but one serious flaw in the bid-the-shape-regardless-of-strength approach is that you can end up floundering at a high level without enough strength to take the tricks to which you are now committed.

Raising partner's minor

You	Partner
1♠	2♣
3♣	

A single raise of responder's minor suit promises at least three cards in support (if you have only three, you should have an honor in the suit).

So after 1♠-2♣, raise to 3♣ with:

♠ A Q 4 3 2   ♥ 4 3   ♦ K 9 8   ♣ A J 4

or

♠ A Q 6 5 3   ♥ 5 4   ♦ 8 2   ♣ A Q 3 2

or

♠ A Q 9 8 7   ♥ A 4   ♦ 8 2   ♣ A Q J 8

but not with:

♠ Q 6 5 4 3   ♥ A J 4   ♦ A 5   ♣ Q 4 3

where 2NT is a better rebid with only three clubs, a balanced minimum and stoppers in unbid suits.

A jump raise of responder's minor is exceedingly rare since it bypasses a possible 3NT contract and it also takes away a lot of bidding space. When used, if ever — I've only held one hand that I thought was appropriate in 25+ years of playing this system — this rebid should show a very distributional hand with 5-card support for responder's suit and a relative minimum in high cards. So, after 1♠-2♣, raise to 4♣ with

♠ A J 8 7 6 4   ♥ 7   ♦ 9   ♣ A Q J 6 3

You are almost 100% sure that the partnership belongs in either spades or clubs.

Raising partner's heart suit

You	Partner
1♠	2♥
?	

Since partner is guaranteeing at least five hearts and enough strength for game, you can set the trump suit when you have at least three hearts. You will also be able to distinguish between hands where a slam is possible and those that will have to settle for game unless partner has substantial extra values. This will be our first exposure to a very important part of the Two-over-One systemic philosophy: **The Principle Of Fast Arrival**.

The Principle Of Fast Arrival means that once we have found our fit and forced to game, then the quicker we get to game, the less interest in slam we have.

The exercise of this principle doesn't necessarily mean the other hand can't carry on, i.e. it is not a 'sign-off'; it just says that the bidder has done his all and it's up to the other hand to supply the extra values that will be needed for a successful slam.

Let's apply this principle to the options for raising partner's heart suit:

♠ A Q 9 8 7 ♥ K Q 3 2 ♦ Q 5 ♣ 8 3

You	Partner
1♠	2♥
4♥	

Following 'fast arrival', you will generally have 4-card support, a minimum opening bid and no side-suit shortness. A splinter raise may be used with any 1♠ opener that has a 4-card fit for hearts and side-suit shortness (singleton or void), via this type of sequence:

♠ A J 7 6 3 ♥ A J 7 6 ♦ 5 ♣ K 7 6

You	Partner
1♠	2♥
4♦	

All other hands with a heart fit (three to an honor or better) will be shown by a raise to 3♥:

♠ A Q 5 4 3 ♥ K J 4 ♦ A 7 2 ♣ 5 4

♠ A Q J 7 4 ♥ K Q 5 2 ♦ A 5 ♣ K 5

Just raise to 3♥ on either of these hands.

Something special — jump rebidding your major

Since you don't need to jump to encourage partner to keep bidding as you used to have to do in Standard, we can assign specialized meanings to these 'unnecessary' jumps. The jump rebid of your own major after a Two-over-One response shows a completely solid six-card suit in a hand that doesn't necessarily have extra values. You are showing partner a 'source of tricks' and strongly suggesting that either the major be trumps or that the hand be played in notrump with the solid suit being counted on for six or more tricks. After this rebid, partner is strongly encouraged either to cuebid or perhaps just to take control and place the contract.

BY THE WAY

There are also two specialized rebids that you can play if you want. (1) 3NT, which shows a near-solid 6-card or longer suit (usually missing only one of the top three honors) in a 6-3-2-2 hand with stoppers in the unbid suits. (2) A rebid of four of your major, which shows a quality suit of 7-8 cards and about 7-8 playing tricks, usually with too much in the way of defensive assets or playing strength to have been opened with a preemptive bid at the three- or four-level.

So, after

You	Partner
1♠	2♣
?	

rebid 3♠ with either of these hands:

♠ A K Q J 7 6 ♥ Q 5 ♦ 7 6 5 ♣ 10 8

♠ A K Q J 6 2 ♥ A 7 6 ♦ K 8 7 ♣ 4

but not with:

♠ A Q J 8 7 6 ♥ A J 7 ♦ K J 7 ♣ 9

where your spade suit is not solid, nor with:

♠ A K Q J 7 ♥ A 6 5 ♦ 6 5 ♣ 8 7 6

where the suit is solid but only five cards long. It's very difficult to take six tricks with a 5-card suit!

A simple rebid in your own suit

Last but not least, in all other instances where you have at least six cards in your major suit, with or without extra values, you will simply rebid it.

BY THE WAY

Occasionally having to rebid your major with only a five card-suit may be the system area where you will have to make the biggest psychological adjustment from Standard thinking. For example, 1♠-2♣-2♠ sounds like a 6-card suit but that won't always be the case. This rebid also sounds like a minimum hand but that often won't be the case either.

Unfortunately, you will also come across many hands where you only have five cards in your major but that don't fit any of the rebids we've talked about. In these instances, you will still have to rebid your suit. Don't worry about this — there are ways to sort it out in the subsequent bidding.

So, after

You	Partner
1♠	2♣
?	

rebid 2♠ with either of these hands:

♠ A Q J 6 5 4 ♥ A J 7 ♦ 7 6 4 ♣ 4

♠ K Q J 5 4 ♥ A 7 6 ♦ 9 8 7 ♣ K 4

And after

You	Partner
1♥	2♦

rebid 2♥ with either of these hands:

♠ Q J 7 6 ♥ A K 8 7 6 ♦ 7 ♣ Q 4 3

♠ A Q J ♥ A Q 10 5 4 3 ♦ A 4 ♣ 6 5

If you have a choice between bidding a new suit or rebidding a 6-card suit at the same level, I recommend you rebid the 6-card suit with a minimum opener and bid the new suit with extra values.

You	*Partner*
1♠	2♣
?	

♠ A Q 6 5 4 3 ♥ K 5 ♦ Q J 7 6 ♣ 4

With this hand rebid 2♠, but with

♠ A Q 7 6 5 4 ♥ K 5 ♦ A Q 4 3 ♣ 6

which is much stronger, rebid 2♦ now and bid more spades later.

The auction continues…

After opener's rebid, responder will generally have a much clearer picture of both the appropriate strain and possible level the partnership belongs in. In order of desirability, he will want to head towards a major-suit fit if appropriate, with notrump as the first alternative and a minor suit as a distant third choice. Except in very rare circumstances, responder should not go out of his way to raise even a rebid major with only 2-card support — there will usually be something else you can do to find out if the rebid suit really is at least six cards in length.

In a marked departure from Standard methods, responder will frequently be able to use a rebid of 2NT as a stalling tactic in order to get more information from opener before placing the contract. In auctions where there has been a clear indication of the desirability of making a particular suit trumps, new suit bids by responder below game should be used as cuebids towards a possible slam.

It bears repeating that any and all bids responder might make below game are still forcing to game — that force was established with the original Two-over-One response. In fact, the slower responder goes, generally the stronger he is! Responder will thus follow the Principle of Fast Arrival when a fit is found to signify his interest, or lack thereof, in a possible slam.

Summary

Opener's possible rebids after a game-forcing Two-over-One response to his 1♥ or 1♠ opening are:

✓ 2NT = either 12-14 HCP, balanced hand, unbid suits stopped or 18-19 HCP, balanced hand, unbid suits stopped.

✓ New suit (not a reverse) = at least four cards with or without extra values

✓ A reverse promises extra values (16+ HCP) with the second suit shorter than the first.

✓ Raise of responder's suit = at least 3 cards (with an honor if only three); 'fast arrival' applies if a 1♠ opener is raising hearts.

✓ Jump in new suit = splinter raise of responder with 4+ trumps, shortness in bid suit.

✓ Jump rebid of opener's own suit = solid suit, at least six long; invites responder to take over and place the contract.

✓ Simple rebid of opener's major = usually a 6-card suit in a hand that doesn't fit any of above categories but may be a 'bid of convenience' with only a 5-card suit.

AFTER A TWO-OVER-ONE RESPONSE

NOW TRY THESE...

The best way to put all this together is with a Step-ending quiz. This time I'm going to give you both hands, and ask you to construct a good Two-over-One auction for each pair.

1

Opener	Responder
♠ A Q 4 3 2	♠ K 8
♥ K 7 3	♥ Q 10 9
♦ J 9 5	♦ A 6 4
♣ K 9	♣ A Q 8 7 6

2

Opener	Responder
♠ K J 10 8 7	♠ A 5
♥ A Q 4	♥ K 8 7
♦ K Q 4	♦ J 10 7
♣ A 6	♣ K Q J 8 7

3

Opener	Responder
♠ A K Q J 9 2	♠ 10 5
♥ 10 8 7	♥ 6
♦ A 5	♦ K Q 6 2
♣ 6 2	♣ A K Q 9 8 5

4

Opener	Responder
♠ A Q J 7 6	♠ K 10 5 4
♥ K J 7 6	♥ 4 2
♦ Q 3	♦ J 7
♣ 7 2	♣ A K Q 10 8

5

Opener	Responder
♠ A J 10 5	♠ K Q 4 2
♥ Q 10 7 6 5	♥ 3
♦ K	♦ A Q J 10 4
♣ A Q J	♣ K 7 6

6

Opener	Responder
♠ A J 8 7 6 5	♠ K Q 3
♥ K 7 6	♥ 5 4
♦ 4 2	♦ K 8 7
♣ A 6	♣ K Q 5 4 3

7

Opener	Responder
♠ A K 10 7 6	♠ Q 4
♥ Q J 6	♥ K 7 5
♦ 4 3	♦ A K Q 8 7 6
♣ Q 4 2	♣ 5 3

8

Opener	Responder
♠ Q J 7 6 5	♠ A 3
♥ A Q 4 3	♥ K J 8 7 6 5 2
♦ K 5 4	♦ A
♣ 2	♣ 9 8 7

9

Opener	Responder
♠ K Q 10 6 5	♠ A 8
♥ A 6 5	♥ K Q 4
♦ A 4	♦ K J 8 7 6
♣ 8 7 6	♣ 9 5 4

10

Opener	Responder
♠ A K 8 7 6	♠ 10 4
♥ A K 8 7 6	♥ Q J 10 9
♦ A 6	♦ K Q 10 7 4
♣ 6	♣ A 4

ANSWERS

1

Opener	Responder
1♠	2♣
2♠[1]	2NT[2]
3NT[3]	pass

1. Rebid of convenience, nothing else fits.
2. Stalling and forcing.
3. Really only five spades, looks like good contract.

2

Opener	Responder
1♠	2♣
2NT[1]	3NT[2]
4NT[3]	6NT[4]
pass	

1. Usually 12-14 HCP, balanced but, as here, may be 18-19 HCP.
2. Looks like a good spot opposite 12-14 HCP.
3. Surprise! I've got the big one! This is a quantitative raise.
4. I accept — 14 HCP with a good 5-card suit should be enough.

3

Opener	Responder
1♠	2♣
3♠[1]	4♣[2]
4♦[3]	5♣[4]
5♠[5]	6♠[6]
pass	

1. Solid suit of 6+cards.
2. Cuebid in support of spades, first-round control.
3. Also first-round control.
4. Continuing to cuebid, can count lots of tricks. Grand slam may be possible if opener has first-round control of hearts.
5. Nothing more to show, I've said it all!
6. That's OK, I can handle hearts after the first round.

4

Opener	Responder
1♠	2♣
2♥[1]	2♠[2]
4♠[3]	pass

1. Natural, at least four hearts, with or without extra values.
2. Very strong spade raise, usually with either extra HCP or a 'source of tricks' — unsuitable for an original Jacoby 2NT.
3. Fast arrival, sorry nothing extra over here!

5

Opener	Responder
1♥	2♦
2♠[1]	3♠[2]
4♣[3]	4♦[4]
5♦[5]	6♠[6]
pass	

1. Reverse, 16+ HCP, longer hearts than spades.
2. Agrees spades, stronger than bidding 4♠ (which would be fast arrival).
3. Cuebid of first-round control, slam-try.
4. Cuebid of first-round control, slam-try.
5. Second-round control.
6. Responder knows opener must be concerned about hearts since he was unable to cuebid them over 4♦ or go on to slam on his own but this is one time shortness in partner's first suit is a good thing!

6

Opener	Responder
1♠	2♣
2♠[1]	4♠[2]
pass	

1. Usually at least six cards in suit but may be 'bid of convenience' with five.
2. Fast arrival. I don't care whether you've got five or six. I've got real support but a minimum hand for my original Two-over-One response.

7

Opener	Responder
1♠	2♦
2NT[1]	3♦[2]
3NT[3]	pass

1. Usually 12-14 HCP, balanced, as here.
2. Really good diamonds, still some mild slam interest.
3. Not me.

8

Opener	Responder
1♠	2♥
4♣[1]	4NT[2]
5♦	6♥
pass	

1. Splinter raise of hearts with 4-card support and club shortness.
2. Great fit, any aces?

9

Opener	Responder
1♠	2♦
2♠[1]	2NT[2]
3♦[3]	3♠[4]
3NT[5]	pass[6]

1. Nothing else fits.
2. Tell me more. This suggests a strain but is also prepared to make delayed raise of spades if possible.
3. Delayed diamond support, three small or a doubleton honor.
4. Delayed spade support (fewer than three).
5. Sorry only five spades, maybe we should play here.
6. Maybe they won't lead clubs or they'll split. The truly paranoid might fear clubs too much and choose to play 4♠ — that's OK too.

10

Opener	Responder
1♠	2♦
2♥[1]	4♥[2]
4NT[3]	5♦
5NT[3]	6♦
7♥[4]	pass

1. At least four hearts, may have extra values (and how!).
2. Fast arrival= minimum Two-over-One response with 4-card heart support.
3. Blackwood
4. Looks good to me, might need a heart split if you don't have the queen. (Yes, the scientists could use Key Card Blackwood to find out about that trump queen!)

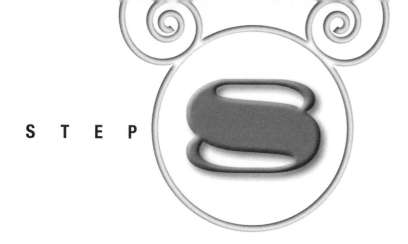

AFTER A MAJOR-SUIT RAISE

> ♥ It is very rare to find hands where slam is makable merely from high cards. *Criticus.* **Contract Simplicitas.** *1933*

Back in Step 4, we saw several ways that you can show immediate support for partner's opening bid of 1♥ or 1♠. When one of those responses has been used, one of the two critical questions of constructive bidding has been answered: we know the partnership is going to play in our agreed-on major suit.

While it may be true that on a rare occasion you might be better off playing in some other suit or even notrump, it hardly bears worrying about. One fit per partnership per deal is usually enough to find and cope with — bidding space and energy have better uses than finding a fit and then rejecting it in favor of looking for some other hypothetically better contract.

Having established the solid base of our major-suit fit, we can proceed from there to search for the proper level — partscore, game or slam. Making this search easier and usually more effective than it is in Standard bidding is the clear description given by each of our various immediate raises.

After a constructive single raise

You	Partner	You	Partner
1♥	2♥	1♠	2♠
?		?	

You know that partner will deliver 3-card support in a hand with 7-10 HCP. In this type of bidding situation, the three-ranges-of-hand classification system you may have encountered elsewhere works well. With a minimum hand, you pass. With an extra-strength hand, you bid directly to game or, in rare circumstances, may even make a move towards slam. The in-between hands will issue some kind of game invitation.

Your first task, then, is first to go through a modest stage of reevaluation in light of the fit that's been established. In addition to your HCP, you can add 2 points for every trump you hold beyond the minimum guaranteed number of five, as well as 2 points for any side suit of five cards. The logic of this is simple: once a fit has been found, extra trumps mean extra tricks just as length in a side suit can mean extra tricks once trumps have been drawn.

For example:

♠ A Q 6 5 4   ♥ 8 7   ♦ A Q J 6 5   ♣ 6

was a 13 HCP 1♠ opening bid. Once raised to 2♠, you add 2 points for the 5-card diamond suit and have a 15-point hand. Having opened 1♠ with

♠ Q J 8 7 6 5   ♥ A 4   ♦ K Q J 5   ♣ 2

you can add 2 extra points (for the sixth trump) when you are raised to 2♠, for a total of 15.

Finished with the process of reevaluation, you are ready to proceed. With a minimum hand in the 12-15 point range, you should pass. In the 17+ point range, you should proceed straight to game without further ado (although we will see some exceptions where you will want to make a below-game slam-try).

The in-between hands, those in the 15-17 total point range, are the hands that are more problematic and will usually only be worth a try for game.

In the early days of bidding, a major-suit opener who was raised to the two-level and wanted to try for game usually did so by bidding his suit one more time. Responder was invited to bid game with a maximum raise or pass and stay in a partial with a minimum. Sadly, this approach didn't take into account the most critical element of suit bidding — fit. More important than the quantity of values jointly held will be where those values are located. A better way to approach this key issue is for opener to identify his likeliest source of losers — if responder's hand fits well enough to look after some or all of those losers, a game contract may succeed. Remember, this process will be aided a great deal because our constructive sin-

BY THE WAY

No, the editor didn't miss an overlap in point ranges. There are 'good' 15-point hands which should at least try for game and there are 'bad' 15-pointers which should be satisfied with a partscore. 'Good' features are extra distributional assets like 6-4 shape (maybe you've heard of '6-4 — bid some more'?) or aces and kings rather than queens and jacks in your side suits.

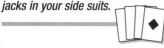

gle raise doesn't include those 5- or 6-point horror-shows you might have felt compelled to raise with in Standard methods.

Our approach is going to address the issue of fit directly. Once you have reevaluated and decided your hand is worth a try for game over partner's raise, you are going to bid the suit in which you need help to cover your identified losers. This method is appropriately called a Help Suit Game Try, or HSGT for short. The suit you make your HSGT in will usually have 2-3 losers and partner is asked to carry on to game in the agreed suit with fitting honors or extreme shortness (like a singleton so that the losers might be ruffed) in the 'help' suit.

Let's look at a couple of examples:

You	Partner #1	You	Partner #2
♠ A Q 6 5 4	♠ K J 7	♠ A Q 6 5 4	♠ K 7 3
♥ J 5 4	♥ 8 7 6 4	♥ J 5 4	♥ K Q 8 3
♦ A K Q 4	♦ 6 5	♦ A K Q 4	♦ 6 5
♣ 3	♣ K J 5 4	♣ 3	♣ 7 6 5 4

You have opened 1♠ and partner has raised to 2♠ on each of the examples shown. Using HSGTs, you would rebid 3♥, saying, 'Do you have any help for my heart losers?' Partner #1 would say 'No' by returning to 3♠ while Partner #2 would say 'Yes, I have heart help' by raising to 4♠. Notice that partner's being minimum or maximum never became an issue — fit was what was being discussed in the bidding conversation.

Notice too that you do not make your game try by rebidding 3♦, your very good side suit, because you don't need any help in that suit — there will be no more than one diamond loser no matter what kind of diamond holding partner has. Psychologically, players often want to 'show' partner they've got really good diamonds in circumstances like this. Don't — it accomplishes nothing!

Before you get too comfortable with this HSGT concept, you pick up

♠ J 8 7 6 4 ♥ A K Q 4 ♦ K Q J ♣ 5

and hear partner raise your 1♠ opening to 2♠. A maximum raise with weak spades may not produce game while a suitable minimum with good trumps will do just fine. What do you do now? Well, you can ask about partner's trumps by rebidding your suit (which is still a HSGT, if you think about it!):

You	Partner
1♠	2♠
3♠	

This says 'Do you have good trumps, partner?' (in the context of having promised only three to begin with). Partner with

♠ 10 5 2 ♥ J 7 ♦ A 6 5 4 ♣ K Q 3 2

signs off by passing while with

♠ K Q 3 ♥ 5 3 ♦ 10 7 6 5 ♣ Q J 8 4

he carries on to game.

BY THE WAY

For more about HSGT, see 25 Bridge Conventions You Should Know *by Barbara Seagram & Marc Smith.*

BY THE WAY

Some players like to use a rebid of 2NT to ask for good trumps and this can work as well. In this context, the rebid of three of the major may be used as a sort of blocking bid, a 'preemptive reraise', intended to make it harder for the opponents to get in. Others like to use 2NT to show a 5-3-3-2 hand with 18-19 HCP, too good for a 1NT opening.

With a really good hand, you may feel there is a possibility for slam if the hands fit well enough, even opposite partner's 7-10 HCP. One way you might find out about this is to make a HSGT bid, ostensibly trying for game and, if the answer you get is satisfactory, proceed instead to slam. You will, of course, be going to game regardless.

You	*Partner*
♠ A K J 10 5 4	♠ Q 8 3
♥ K 9 2	♥ 10 7 6
♦ A K Q	♦ 7 6 5
♣ 3	♣ A Q 4 2
1♠	2♠
3♥	3♠
4♠	

When asked for heart help, partner says, 'No help, sorry' by returning to 3♠, and you carry on to game anyway.

You	*Partner*
♠ A K J 10 5 4	♠ Q 8 3
♥ K 9 2	♥ A Q 4 3
♦ A K Q	♦ 7 6 5
♣ 3	♣ 10 9 8
1♠	2♠
3♥	4♠
4NT	5♦
6♠	

This time partner says 'Good heart help over here' by bidding game, so you check for aces via Blackwood and bid the slam.

After a Bergen 3♦ limit raise

You	Partner	You	Partner
1♥	3♦	1♠	3♦
?		?	

Mostly due to the level of this response, your choices of rebids are somewhat limited:

1) **Stay in a partscore** by signing off in three of the major. This should only happen when you have a balanced minimum hand of 12-13 poor points (a lot of queens and jacks with 5-3-3-2 distribution), like the following:

   ♠ Q 8 7 6 4   ♥ A Q 3   ♦ K 4   ♣ Q 6 4

2) **Go directly to game** — this is by far the most frequent rebid opposite the limit raise. Remember, partner is promising four trumps so the always

important Ninth Trump will be present. On this hand, just bid 4♠ over partner's 3♦:

♠ Q 8 7 6 4　♥ A Q 3　♦ K Q 4 3　♣ 6

3) **_Occasionally, you will want to try for slam._** You can do so by simply bidding a new suit (as a cuebid).

♠ A Q J 10 4　♥ 6　♦ Q J 7 4　♣ A K 5

You	Partner
1♠	3♦
4♣	

Partner can look at his hand and decide whether to cooperate with your slam try or simply sign off in game.

After a Bergen 3♣ constructive raise

You	Partner	You	Partner
1♥	3♣	1♠	3♣
?		?	

Again due to space restrictions, you don't have a lot of options with regard to inviting game. Basically your choices with regard to game will be simply to bid it or not! Knowing the ninth trump is present will help make the decision somewhat easier and familiarity with the method will also help. Basically, you should proceed to game any time your hand revalues to anything in the 15+ point range, particularly if you have any positive distributional features. The total HCP count between the two hands may not turn out to be the 25 or 26 you've thought you needed for game but, surprisingly, the tricks will be there more often than not!

You	Partner
♠ A Q J 10 3	♠ K 8 7 6
♥ K 8 7	♥ 9 5 2
♦ A 7 6	♦ 9 2
♣ 4 2	♣ K Q 8 3
1♠	3♣
3♠	pass

With a shapeless minimum, you sign off in 3♠ and, on a bad day, may not even make that.

You	Partner
♠ A K 7 6 5	♠ J 8 4 2
♥ K 8 5 2	♥ 9 4 3
♦ A Q 4	♦ 9 2
♣ 8	♣ A K 9 2
1♠	3♣
4♠	pass

With a reasonable hand you carry on to a game that might not make but has lots of chances, possibly aided by the fact that the opening leader will be 'in the dark'. The ninth trump is what makes the aggressively-bid game likely to succeed even though partner has a poor-fitting minimum.

After a preemptive double raise

You	Partner		You	Partner
1♥	3♥		1♠	3♠
?			?	

Keep in mind that the double raises are largely obstructive maneuvers designed to make things difficult for the opponents. You will need a veritable mountain of a hand to bid on to game. Even if you have extra HCP, the hands may do well to produce nine tricks, much less ten (remember some of the hands I suggested making the preemptive raise on in Step 4!). Get used to going down after a preemptive raise. However, it's not a matter to lose any sleep over since (a) you will rarely be doubled for penalties as the defense will not usually have the comfort of trump tricks, and (b) they will almost certainly have a makable and more profitable contract of their own that your auction has not allowed them to find.

You should only bid on if four-plus trumps in the dummy and maybe one outside high card will be enough to make game. Vulnerability will have some bearing on your decision-making as a non-vulnerable preemptive raise can be a truly awful hand — for example

♠ J 5 4 3　♥ 10 2　♦ 9 8 7 6　♣ 10 9 2

while a vulnerable perpetrator of the bid might have a little more:

♠ J 5 4 3　♥ K 5　♦ 9 8 7 6　♣ 10 9 2

Thus, playing strength rather than just HCP should be what you think about.

Here's a hand on which you should take one more bid:

♠ A Q 7 6 5 2　♥ A J 8 5 2　♦ 5 2　♣ —

You have very little in the way of HCP but a lot of playing strength. Knowing dummy will have at least four spades, either long or short hearts in partner's hand will help get that suit established.

And on this hand:

♠ K Q 8 7 6　♥ K 4　♦ A K J 4　♣ K 10

any bits and pieces partner has will help you — you just have too much high-card strength to pass.

After a direct game raise

You	Partner		You	Partner
1♥	4♥		1♠	4♠
?			?	

In the vast majority of cases where partner raises your 1♥ or 1♠ opening directly to game, your assignment will be to pass and hope to make at least ten tricks! Dummy will provide at least five trumps, fewer than 10 HCP and some distributional help, so your prospects of making game should be better than if partner had made a preemptive 3♥ or 3♠ raise.

However, the direct game raise is not a strict 'close out' or sign-off bid in the same vein as a call of 3NT is in response to a 1NT opening. With possible slam prospects, you may proceed — with extreme caution — although the level the auction has arrived at puts severe limitations on the possible ways you can issue a slam invitation.

♠ A K Q 3 2 ♥ A K 8 7 6 ♦ K 5 ♣ 4

Here you have reasonable expectations of being able to make slam if partner has an ace to go with his five or more trumps, so just use Blackwood now to find out. It's also not unreasonable to hope that partner's distributional assets might include heart shortness.

♠ A K 10 5 4 3 ♥ — ♦ Q 3 ♣ A Q 8 7 6

This time you need partner to have a specific ace, the ace of diamonds, something you can't find out via Blackwood, so start a cuebidding sequence with 5♣. If partner cuebids diamonds, you will go on to slam; otherwise, you'll shut things down at the five-level.

♠ A Q J 7 6 ♥ K Q J 10 5 ♦ Q 3 ♣ K

This time, while you have lots of HCP, you would need more controls from partner than you have any reason to expect, so you should be content just to play in game.

After a Jacoby 2NT

You	Partner		You	Partner
1♥	2NT		1♠	2NT
?			?	

After the conventional 2NT response, (a) the auction cannot stop below game and (b) slam may be possible if you have a good fit and enough strength between the two hands.

Your possible rebids are as follows:

4 of your major	The weakest possible rebid showing a minimum hand (12-14 HCP) and no side suit shortness.
3 of your major	No side suit shortness but a hand seriously interested in slam — usually 17+ HCP.
3NT	No shortness but about a king more than a minimum and some slam interest (15-17 HCP but not a balanced hand as you would have opened 1NT in the first place).
3 of a new suit	Singleton or void in the bid suit.
4 a new suit	A good 5+card second suit. The idea here is that, if partner has a fitting honor and controls in the other two suits, slam will be very easy.

If your rebid suits partner's hand, he may cuebid or perhaps just take control with Blackwood. Alternatively, a return to the agreed trump suit at the three-level (if available) is strong and invites you to cuebid. A rebid of four of your major by partner is a sign-off.

After a splinter bid

After a splinter bid, which shows shortness in the suit bid along with game-going values and at least 4-card trump support, you have to evaluate slam prospects in light of partner's shortness. Blackwood or cuebidding may be used to further explore the slam prospects but, as in all shortness-showing auctions, you should be wary of wasted values in the announced short suit.

You	Partner
♠ A Q J 7 6	♠ K 8 5 4
♥ A Q 4	♥ K 10 6 5
♦ 9 7 6 5	♦ 3
♣ K	♣ A J 8 5
1♠	4♦
4NT	5♦
6♠	

You know after the 4♦ splinter raise that your hands fit extremely well. You check on controls via Blackwood and place the contract. Note that partner has an absolute minimum but that you will be able to ruff two of your losing diamonds and discard the fourth almost regardless of what the defense can do. And all this on a combined 27 HCP!

Summary

✓ After auctions that start one of a major followed by an immediate raise, you are almost always going to play in that major.

✓ After a single raise, opener may sign off, bid game directly, or try for game by bidding a new suit in which he needs help (HSGT).

✓ After a Bergen limit raise (3♦) opener should bid at least game unless he is 5-3-3-2 with a bad minimum.

✓ After a Bergen 4-card constructive raise (3♣) sign off at three of the major with a minimum hand, otherwise bid game directly.

✓ A very strong hand in HCP or distributional playing strength is needed to bid a game opposite a preemptive raise — if you're intending to make it!

✓ Stop! — usually, after a direct game raise.

✓ Opener's rebids show strength and/or shape after a Jacoby 2NT raise.

✓ After Jacoby raises and splinter bids, use the 30-point deck concept to help evaluate slam prospects.

A F T E R   A   M A J O R - S U I T   R A I S E

NOW TRY THESE...

On each of the following hands, you've opened 1♠. What is your rebid opposite the indicated response from partner?

♠ A Q 6 5 4	**1**	2♠	
♥ K J 9 7	**2**	3♣	
♦ A 5	**3**	3♦	
♣ 7 6	**4**	3♠	
	5	4♠	
	6	2NT	
	7	4♥	

♠ K J 10 9 5 4	**8**	2♠	
♥ 8 7 6	**9**	3♣	
♦ A K Q	**10**	3♦	
♣ 6	**11**	3♠	
	12	4♠	
	13	2NT	
	14	4♣	

♠ A K 5 4 3 2	**15**	2♠	
♥ A K Q 2	**16**	3♣	
♦ 5 3	**17**	3♦	
♣ 6	**18**	3♠	
	19	4♠	
	20	2NT	
	21	4♥	

ANSWERS

1 Pass   Game prospects are not good.

2 3♣   Not enough for game opposite a 4-card constructive raise. Don't forget to 'return' to the agreed suit — if you sign off by passing, clubs will be trumps. Don't laugh, it happens to Bergen players all the time!

3 4♠   A little more than a minimum and a bit of shape — enough for game opposite a limit raise.

4 Pass   Hope you can come close to making nine tricks.

5 Pass   Game is enough.

6 4♠   A minimum, albeit respectable, so that if there are any slam moves to be made, partner will have to be the initiator.

7 4♠   Too much wastage in partner's splinter suit to make any slam moves.

8 3♥   Ask for help in hearts — there may be a good-fitting game!

9 4♠   Enough extra playing strength to bid game.

10 4♠   You certainly want to be in game, but slam is unlikely (although certainly not impossible).

11 P/4♠   This time both actions have a roughly equal chance of being right. It's probably best to pass non-vulnerable and bid on vulnerable, when you can expect just a smidgin more from across the table.

12 Pass   Certainly not enough for a slam adventure.

13 3♣   Show your singleton and go from there.

14 4♦   You might not believe that partner also has shortness in clubs but it does happen. Cuebid and see what happens next.

15 4♠   Not many losers in view.

16 4♠   Enough for game, not likely for more than that.

17 4♠   Game for sure — slam if partner has just the right cards so you might even make a try with 3♥ and see what happens.

18 4♠   Playing strength, not HCP, justify this. Partner could have just the four little trumps he's promised and nary a picture card and you'd still be a favorite to take ten tricks.

19 Pass   Enough already.

20 3♣   Show your singleton. Not enough length (five cards required) to show the second suit.

21 4NT   A lot of wastage opposite partner's shortness in hearts but many reasonable minimums will still produce a slam. You can use Blackwood with a worthless doubleton because you know that partner will have something in diamonds.

AFTER A FORCING 1NT

♥ A successful contract depends on the accurate rebidding of the opening and responding hand. It is here that most average players show lack of knowledge or judgment. **Dudley Courtenay. The System the Experts Play. 1934.**

You	Partner
1♥ *or* 1♠	1NT
?	

As I'm sure you will remember from Step 5, if your (unpassed) partner bids 1NT over your major-suit opening, that call is forcing; you have to bid at least once more. Partner will usually have 5-12 HCP (more in exceptional cases) and may on occasion have concealed support for your major suit. With your first rebid, you will be attempting to provide further information about the strength and shape of your hand. Partner will then usually have a very good idea of where the hand should be played. His general obligations will include letting you know if there is a fit for a trump suit. He must also tell you whether the combined values will be sufficient for game or slam or perhaps that you should be content with a partscore.

AFTER A FORCING 1NT

Most of your possible rebids have very similar meanings to those that you will have been used to in Standard methods, but some will differ a little bit, while one particular type of hand will be treated in a markedly different fashion. Let's take a look at the options at your disposal, and see how the auction is likely to develop.

Which rebids are basically unchanged?

1) A simple rebid of your major

You	Partner
1♠	1NT
2♠	

This promises at least six cards in the major suit and a minimum strength hand (12-15 HCP – maybe 11 HCP if you were a bit adventuresome with your opening bid). Here's a typical hand for this rebid:

♠ A J 10 6 5 4　♥ A K 5　♦ 8 7 6　♣ 5

Let's take a look at some of the ways the auction can go on from here. Partner should pass with a nondescript minimum hand (5-8 HCP) like this one:

♠ 4 3　♥ Q 7 6 5　♦ K J 8 7　♣ J 9 6

You	Partner
1♠	1NT
2♠	pass

A hand with real support that was too weak for an immediate raise should also usually pass with only three trumps:

♠ J 7 6　♥ K Q 4 3　♦ 9 7 6 5　♣ 10 2

You	Partner
1♠	1NT
2♠	pass

However, partner might chance a raise with 4-card support in a hand that was in between the strengths for any of the immediate raises:

♠ 9 7 6 5　♥ A Q 3 2　♦ 9 2　♣ 7 6 2

You	Partner
1♠	1NT
2♠	3♠

He should also raise invitationally with 9-12 HCP and two trumps (since you have found at least an 8-card fit):

♠ 6 5　♥ A 6 5　♦ K Q 5 4　♣ Q 8 7 6

You	Partner
1♠	1NT
2♠	3♠

With 10-12 HCP with 3-card support (a 3-card limit raise), there is a proven 9-card fit and enough high-card points between you to take a shot at game. Partner should raise directly to game — without passing GO or collecting $200!

♠ A J 4　♥ K 8 7 6　♦ K 7 6 5　♣ 4 2

You	Partner
1♠	1NT
2♣	4♠

Finally, if partner has a weak unbalanced hand with a long suit, trying to improve the contract will usually be a lost cause; since your major suit is known to be at least six cards long, generally the best action is to pass and hope!

♠ 7　♥ Q 8 7　♦ 4 3 2　♣ K J 9 5 4 2

You	Partner
1♠	1NT
2♠	pass

2) A simple rebid of a new suit

You	Partner
1♠	1NT
2♦	

This usually shows at least 4 cards in the new suit and 12-17 HCP. Either of the hands shown would fit the auction:

♠ A J 6 5 4　♥ K Q 3　♦ Q 7 6 5　♣ 9

♠ A Q 10 5 2　♥ 5　♦ A K J 3 2　♣ 4 3

This new-suit rebid is not forcing but, as we shall see later, if the new suit is a minor, you may have as few as three cards in the suit. Let's look at some examples of how the auction might continue.

If partner is weak and nondescript, he should usually take a simple preference back to the major with two cards in support:

♠ 7 2　♥ Q 8 7 6　♦ 9 4 2　♣ K J 9 8

You	Partner
1♠	1NT
2♦	2♠

With a weak 3- or 4-card raise for your major, partner also takes a simple preference back to that major, but will be a little happier doing so:

♠ J 9 8　♥ K 8 5 3　♦ 5 2　♣ Q 9 7 5

You	Partner
1♠	1NT
2♦	2♠

However, with good support for your minor, or fewer than two cards in your major, he will pass with a weak hand. Here he passes 2♦, since at least an 8-card fit has been found:

♠ 6 2　♥ Q 8 2　♦ 9 7 6 4 2　♣ K J 8

You	Partner
1♠	1NT
2♦	pass

Partner passes again here — nothing else appeals and maybe you will be kind enough to have at least four diamonds:

♠ 6　♥ Q J 6 5　♦ K 9 7 6　♣ 7 6 3 2

You	Partner
1♠	1NT
2♦	pass

With the 10-12 HCP 3-card limit raise type of hand, partner takes a jump preference to show real support and invitational values:

♠ A J 6　♥ K 8 7 4　♦ 9 2　♣ K 9 3 2

You	Partner
1♠	1NT
2♦	3♠

BY THE WAY

On rare occasions, partner will have an awkward rebid with an invitational hand, and may have to 'fudge' either a stopper or a card in support.

With the weak unbalanced type of hand, partner may ask you to allow him to play in his own long suit. Partner will have little or no tolerance for your major, as in this case:

♠ 5　♥ Q 8 7 6 4 3　♦ 7 5　♣ K 5 4 2

You	Partner
1♠	1NT
2♦	2♥

Of course, if you've already hit partner's long suit, then with a weak hand he can pass and go out to buy a lottery ticket(!):

♠ 7　♥ Q 4　♦ K 8 7 6 4 3　♣ 9 6 4 3

You	Partner
1♠	1NT
2♦	pass

With balanced or semi-balanced invitational strength, partner can rebid 2NT (invitational) when he has both unbid suits stopped:

♠ 5 3　♥ A J 8 7　♦ Q 6 5　♣ K J 8 7

You	Partner
1♠	1NT
2♦	2NT

Partner is also allowed to raise your second suit. In order to raise, he should usually have at least five cards if your second suit is a minor, but four is sufficient support for hearts since a 1♠ opener who rebids 2♥ will have at least four of them for that action:

♠ 5 3   ♥ A 10 6 5   ♦ K Q J 6 3   ♣ 10 4

You	Partner
1♠	1NT
2♦	3♦

3) A single jump rebid of your major

This promises at least six cards in the major suit and a medium-strength hand (15-18 HCP) that wants to invite to game (usually in the major suit but occasionally in notrump). For example:

♠ A Q J 9 8 7   ♥ A   ♦ K Q 7   ♣ 7 5 3

You	Partner
1♠	1NT
3♠	

How will the auction continue? Partner should pass with any poor 5-8 HCP hand and no fit. In fact, even if he has his own long suit he must pass and make the best of it, because bidding a new suit now would be a slam try (see below). He shouldn't worry about not having much support – your jump rebid is supposed to show a good quality suit. He should pass on either of the hands shown, therefore:

♠ 5   ♥ Q 4 3   ♦ K J 9 8 6 4 3   ♣ 3 2

♠ 4 3   ♥ K 8 7 6 5   ♦ Q J 6   ♣ 8 5 4

You	Partner
1♠	1NT
3♠	pass

With the 'weak raise' type of hand, partner should also normally refuse the invitation:

♠ J 6 5   ♥ 10 2   ♦ K 8 7 6 4   ♣ Q 4 3

You	Partner
1♠	1NT
3♠	pass

He should go on to game, however, on the rare occasion when his weak raise includes positive features like a ruffing value or a side-suit ace, especially if he has 4-card support:

♠ 9 7 6 5   ♥ A Q 4 3   ♦ 10 2   ♣ 10 4 3

You	Partner
1♠	1NT
3♠	4♠

With the 3-card limit raise type hand, partner knows there is a fit and values sufficient for at least game so with an average hand of this variety, partner raises to game:

♠ 976 ♥ K Q 5 4 ♦ K 7 ♣ Q J 6 5

You	Partner
1♠	1NT
3♠	4♠

With a very good hand (aces and kings plus ruffing value) partner can try for slam with an advance cuebid, the bid of a new suit that in this instance says, 'I like your suit and have first-round control of the suit I'm bidding on the way to game.'

♠ A 4 3 ♥ K 6 5 ♦ 10 2 ♣ A 8 7 6 5

You	Partner
1♠	1NT
3♠	4♣

With a balanced, semi-balanced or even unbalanced hand in the invitational range (9-12 HCP) partner should accept the invitation posed by your jump rebid. Remember, he doesn't need a lot of support for your major since you promise a quality suit:

♠ 3 2 ♥ A 7 6 5 ♥ K 7 6 5 4 ♣ K 6

You	Partner
1♠	1NT
3♠	4♠

However, he should try to have something resembling a stopper in all unbid suits to bid 3NT:

♠ 3 2 ♥ K J 9 2 ♦ Q J 9 4 ♣ K J 7

You	Partner
1♠	1NT
3♠	3NT

4) A jump to game in your major

You	Partner
1♠	1NT
4♠	

A rare rebid on a very good 7+ card suit in a hand with about 7½ to 8½ playing tricks that would need a lot of aces and kings from partner to be able to make a slam. This type of hand will not have been strong enough for a game-forcing 2♣ opening and will usually have a combination of more playing strength and side-suit strength than a four-of-a-major opening would usually deliver. You might have one of these hands for this auction:

♠ K Q J 7 6 5 4 ♥ 6 ♦ K Q 4 ♣ A 4
♠ A K J 10 4 3 2 ♥ — ♦ Q J 6 ♣ K J 4

Partner will rarely want to make any further move in the auction. While it isn't strictly what you might call a 'drop dead' bid, the only reason for keeping the auction going will be to investigate a possible slam in your suit. To advance towards slam, partner will need control cards — aces and kings in the side suits.

5) A jump shift

Forcing to game, just as it used to be — a hand that has 18+ HCP, usually unbalanced, with 4+ cards in the second suit. The second suit should never be longer than the first (of course, it may be the same length). Either of these hands would qualify after a 1♠ opening:

♠ A Q J 10 4   ♥ A Q   ♦ K Q J 5 4   ♣ 6

♠ A K J 3 2   ♥ K 6 5   ♦ A K J 4   ♣ 5

You	Partner
1♠	1NT
3♦	

Partner's duty now is to help select the strain in which the game (or possibly slam) will be played. The first ticklish situation will occur when partner has to take a preference to your first suit without real support simply because he has no other clear action available, as here:

♠ 5 3   ♥ 6 5 4   ♦ 9 6 4   ♣ K Q J 4 2

You	Partner
1♠	1NT
3♦	3♠

What complicates this matter somewhat is that a preference to 3♠ is also the right systemic move with the 10-12 HCP 3-card limit raise type of hand, like this one:

♠ K J 7   ♥ K 7 6 5 4   ♦ A 6 5   ♣ 6 3

You	Partner
1♠	1NT
3♦	3♠

Not to worry! Your usual third bid after such a start will be a control- or shape-showing below-game slam try. With the first hand partner will sign off in game, while with the second, he will co-operate. This is obviously a very large subject that will warrant further discussion later on.

When partner has the weak raise type of hand he makes use of 'fast arrival' to show a minimum hand with a fit:

♠ J 8 7   ♥ K 8 7 6   ♦ 6 5 4   ♣ Q 5 4

You	Partner
1♠	1NT
3♦	4♠

With stoppers in the unbid suits and no great liking for either of your suits, partner might try to place the contract in 3NT — for example with this hand:

♠ 6 5　♥ Q J 6 5　♦ J 7 6　♣ K Q 5 4

You	Partner
1♠	1NT
3♦	3NT

6) *A reverse to 2♠ after an opening bid of 1♥*

You	Partner
1♥	1NT
2♠	

This sequence promises at least four spades and 16+ HCP. (Note that your spades should always be shorter than your hearts.) With only four spades, you are mainly concerned with showing the size and shape of your hand — partner won't have four spades since he bid 1NT not 1♠ in the first place. As is always the case with reverses, this rebid is forcing for one round.

Typical hands would be either of these:

♠ A Q J 5　♥ A K Q 4 3　♦ Q 3　♣ 5 2

♠ A K J 6 5　♥ A K J 10 4 3　♦ 6　♣ 7

but not these:

♠ A J 7 6　♥ K J 4 3 2　♦ 7　♣ K 8 7

♠ A Q 7 6 5　♥ A K Q 6 5　♦ Q 3　♣ 3

The first example is too weak to reverse, while the second is the wrong shape – with this hand you should have opened 1♠ in the first place.

After you reverse, partner's duty will be to show a fit for hearts if possible or to steer the contract towards notrump otherwise. I will deal with this situation in greater depth in Step 22 but here are some possible rebids by partner:

♠ 7 6　♥ Q 6 5　♦ K Q 4 3　♣ 8 6 5 4

You	Partner
1♥	1NT
2♠	3♥

Partner shows a weak raise.

♠ 7 6　♥ A J 7　♦ K 8 7 6　♣ K 5 4 3

You	Partner
1♥	1NT
2♠	4♥

Partner has a 3-card limit raise.

♠ 7 5　♥ 8 7　♦ Q 10 6 4　♣ K Q 6 5 4

You	Partner
1♥	1NT
2♠	2NT

Partner shows a minimum with no fit.

♠ 65 ♥ 76 ♦ Q J 7 6 ♣ K Q J 6 5

You	Partner
1♥	1NT
2♣	3NT

Partner has just enough to bid game.

Which rebids are slightly different?

1) A 2NT rebid

You	Partner
1♥ *or* 1♠	1NT
2NT	

This shows 18-19 HCP in a balanced hand. This rebid almost creates a game force but it allows partner room to show support for your major, bid a long suit of his own or even pass 2NT with a truly awful hand (5-6 HCP) for his initial response. Either of these hands would rebid 2NT after 1♠-1NT:

♠ K J 10 4 3 ♥ A 3 ♦ A Q 3 ♣ K J 5

♠ A J 7 6 5 ♥ Q 3 ♦ K Q J ♣ A Q 4

Since the 2NT rebid is essentially an invitation to game based on 18-19 HCP in a balanced hand, partner's choices will be to:

- *Accept the invitation* by bidding game immediately in either notrump or your suit. For the first option, partner should have about 7+ HCP with no support for the major while a jump to game in the major is made with the 10-12 HCP 3-card limit raise type of hand.

- *Show a weak raise* by reverting to three of the major. You may or may not go on to game based on how well you like your hand in light of the announced fit.

- *Sign off in three of his own long suit* with a weak hand (usually it's a weak long suit because otherwise it might be worth a lot of tricks in notrump).

- *Pass* with a complete dog.

Here are some examples of what partner might bid over 2NT:

♠ 4 3 ♥ 9 8 7 ♦ K Q 8 7 6 ♣ 9 4 2

You	Partner
1♠	1NT
2NT	pass

♠ 4 3 ♥ Q 8 7 ♦ K Q 8 7 6 ♣ 9 4 2

You	Partner
1♠	1NT
2NT	3NT

♠ A J 7　♥ Q 7 6 5　♦ K J 6 5　♣ 5 4

You	Partner
1♠	1NT
2NT	4♠

♠ J 4 3　♥ K Q 8 4　♦ 6 5 3 2　♣ 6 2

You	Partner
1♠	1NT
2NT	3♠

♠ 3　♥ Q 5 4　♦ Q 5　♣ J 9 7 6 5 3 2

You	Partner
1♠	1NT
2NT	3♣

♠ 7　♥ A Q 9 7 5 4　♦ 8 7 6　♣ 6 5 2

You	Partner
1♠	1NT
2NT	4♥

2)　A 3NT rebid

You	Partner
1♥ *or* 1♠	1NT
3NT	

This is rare and shows a 'source of tricks' type of hand: a very good 6+ cards in your major, usually solid or nearly so, in a semi-balanced hand (no singletons or voids) of 17-19 HCP with at least two of the three side suits stopped. You expect to make 3NT opposite many very minimum hands largely because of the tricks that can be taken with this hand. This might be called a strong semi-gambling rebid.

After 1♠-1NT, 3NT would be the rebid with either of these hands:

♠ A K Q 10 9 4　♥ A 4　♦ Q J 5　♣ K 10

♠ K Q J 10 9 4　♥ K J 5　♦ A 3　♣ A 3

Partly because of the high level this rebid occurs at, partner's options are somewhat limited. He can:

- **Pass** with any hand that has no fit -– looking for a fit in a different suit at this level will usually be a fruitless exercise.

- **Convert to four of your major** with either the weak raise or an unexceptional 3-card limit raise.

- **Make a cuebid** to show a control, a good 3-card limit raise and some slam interest.

So which rebid is a dramatic change from Standard?

Keeping in mind that opener always has to make some kind of rebid after the Forcing 1NT response, there are (sadly) hands that just don't fit any of the above categories of rebids. These will usually be balanced hands with no sixth card in the major or no second four-card suit to bid, such as

♠ A Q 4 3 2   ♥ K 5   ♦ J 7 6   ♣ K 5 4

You have held hands like this, haven't you? A similar problem occurs when you have

♠ A J 6 5   ♥ K J 7 6 5   ♦ 5   ♣ A 3 2

and partner responds 1NT to your 1♥ opening. You don't have a sixth heart to rebid 2♥ and a 2♠ bid would be a reverse promising more strength than you have.

Then you might have

♠ A K Q   ♥ K Q J 5 4   ♦ 4 3   ♣ 8 7 3

and have decided (reasonably) not to open 1NT with two unstopped suits. However, you aren't strong enough to rebid 2NT (18-19 HCP) over partner's 1NT and 2♥ would promise a sixth card that you don't have.

In all of these instances, you will make what is called a 'rebid of convenience' — you will rebid your lower three-card minor. In other words, all three of the hands above will rebid 2♣. Keep in mind that (as I hinted above) this now means that an opener's rebid of two of a minor no longer promises at least four cards. but rather a minimum of three. It's just part of the modern trend to show disrespect for the minor suits!

I described earlier how the auction would continue after your new suit rebid, and nothing has changed. As I indicated above, partner will be aware that a minor-suit rebid could only be three cards long, and will rarely pass you there without five of them himself.

Summary

After partner replies to one of a major opening with a Forcing 1NT, your possible rebids are:

✓ Two of your major with 6+ cards and 12-15 HCP.

✓ Three of your major with 6+ cards and 16-18 HCP in an unbalanced hand.

✓ Four of your major with 7½-8½ playing tricks.

✓ Two of a new suit — 4+ cards if a major and 3+ if a minor. This normally shows 12-17 HCP. However, 1♥-1NT-2♠ is a reverse, and promises 16+ HCP.

✓ A jump shift — 18+ HCP and enough overall playing strength to force to game.

✓ 2NT with 18-19 HCP and a balanced hand.

✓ 3NT with a 'source of tricks' in a semi-balanced hand and some outside stoppers.

Partner's follow-up responsibilities will include:

✓ Showing a fit for your major whenever possible.

✓ Ensuring the partnership gets to the appropriate level in light of what he knows about your strength.

AFTER A FORCING 1NT

NOW TRY THESE...

What is your next bid on each of the following auctions?

1 ♠ K 9 8 7 5 4 2
♥ A 6 5
♦ A Q
♣ 6

You	Partner
1♠	1NT
?	

2 ♠ K J 8 7 4
♥ A K
♦ K Q 6 5
♣ 7 6

You	Partner
1♠	1NT
?	

3 ♠ K Q 9 6 4
♥ 9 7
♦ A Q 4
♣ J 7 6

You	Partner
1♠	1NT
?	

4 ♠ K Q J 7 6
♥ A K Q 7 6
♦ 8 2
♣ 9

You	Partner
1♠	1NT
?	

5 ♠ A Q J 10 6 5
♥ A 5
♦ Q J 10
♣ K J

You	Partner
1♠	1NT
?	

6 ♠ A Q 6 5 4
♥ 7
♦ 8 7
♣ A Q 6 5 3

You	Partner
1♠	1NT
?	

7 ♠ A J 10 6 5 4
♥ 7
♦ A Q
♣ A K Q 8

You	Partner
1♠	1NT
?	

8 ♠ A Q 8 6 5
♥ K 6
♦ A 6
♣ K Q 7 6

You	Partner
1♠	1NT
?	

9 ♠ A Q 8 7 6 4
♥ K Q J 5
♦ A 6
♣ 8

You	Partner
1♠	1NT
?	

10 ♠ A K Q J 6
♥ 8 6 5 4
♦ 8
♣ A K Q

You	Partner
1♠	1NT
?	

1   2♠   Extra spade length but poor quality and not enough HCP to justify stronger action.

2   2♦   Some extra strength but not enough to do more. Make the quiet, natural rebid and wait to hear more from partner.

3   2♣   The forced rebid of convenience. Don't make the mistake of bidding 2♦ because the diamonds are so much better. Just as an opener prefers to open 1♣ with 3-3 in the minors so too does an opener rebid 2♣ with 3-3 when nothing else is available.

4   2♥   Some extra values but nothing worth more than a simple natural rebid.

5   2NT   A real toughie! You could make a case for each of 2NT, 3NT or 3♠. The spade suit isn't totally solid so 3NT carries some risk but the outside stoppers show some promise for notrump while the 3♠ rebid would normally be made on a more unbalanced hand. Partners will often differ in their opinions in such cases but I would choose the compromise rebid of 2NT — it puts notrump in the picture without overstating the case for playing in spades. Second prize to 3NT, a slightly more aggressive rebid.

6   ??   You know there's always going to be one question to try to trick you and this is it! You should have opened 1♣ in the first place with a minimum hand and 5-5 in the blacks – check back to Step 2. If you just came back to the table and a kibitzer had opened 1♠ in your place, you would try to recover by rebidding 2♣.

7   3♣   Jump shift to establish a game force and try to sort out in what strain the game should be played.

8   2NT   This comes closest to describing this semi-balanced 18 HCP with stoppers in the unbid suits.

9   2♥   With six spades and four hearts the recommended procedure is to rebid 2♠ with very minimum hands and then, if given a third chance, bid the hearts. With a medium hand like this one, bid hearts at your second turn saving a third bid of spades as a way of showing the extra strength. You might alter this approach if the six spades were very poor and the four hearts were very good.

10   3♣   Probably the best way to describe your game-forcing strength and show 'where you live' in terms of your high cards. A jump shift in the emaciated heart suit certainly isn't appealing and a 2NT or 3NT rebid will mislead partner. The 3♣ rebid will be unlikely to get him to rebid 3NT without red-suit stoppers, which is just what you want!

S T E P **10**

OTHER AUCTIONS
STARTING 1♥ OR 1♠

♥ My bidding is not so unorthodox as would appear at first sight.
Criticus. **Contract Simplicitas.** *1933.*

There are a few auctions left to talk about that start with one of a major but do not involve a Game Forcing Two-over-One response. First there are those which start

You	Partner
1♥	1♠
?	

With a few small refinements, these auctions will be very familiar to you as many of your possible rebids will be the same ones you would make over a Forcing 1NT response. Let's therefore concentrate on the others.

1) 1NT

This shows 12-14 HCP in a balanced hand and may on occasion not have all unbid suits unstopped. Of course, you would prefer to have stoppers but it's not always practical. For example, with

♠ A 5 ♥ K J 7 6 5 ♦ A 5 4 ♣ 10 7 6

a rebid of 1NT is the most descriptive rebid to show the size and shape of the hand even though clubs (remember, who cares about clubs?) are unstopped.

2) Two of a new suit

This time you promise at least four cards in your suit (not a mere three as over the Forcing 1NT) and 12-17 HCP. This is because you now have a 1NT rebid available to deal with those minimum 5-3-3-2 hands.

3) A spade raise

Perish the thought, but you may have support for partner's spades and can show it directly:

♠ A Q 4 3　♥ K Q 6 5 4　♦ J 7　♣ 5 4

You	Partner
1♥	1♠
2♠	

4-card support, minimum hand (may on rare occasion have only 3-card support).

♠ A Q 4 2　♥ K Q 6 5 4　♦ A 6　♣ Q 4

You	Partner
1♥	1♠
3♠	

Strongly invitational with four spades and 16-18 HCP.

♠ A Q 4 2　♥ K Q 6 5 4　♦ A 6　♣ A 4

You	Partner
1♥	1♠
4♠	

Enough strength for game (18-20 HCP), 4-card support and no side-suit shortness.

♠ A Q 4 2　♥ K Q 6 5 4　♦ A K 6　♣ 5

You	Partner
1♥	1♠
4♣	

A splinter raise of spades, showing 4-card support, game-going strength and shortness in clubs (this is why the raise to 4♠ denies shortness).

Other responses to 1♥ or 1♠

1) A jump shift in the other major

You may have noticed (especially if you're not reading the 'By The Way' features very carefully) that we have not yet discussed two auctions:

Partner	You		Partner	You
1♠	3♥		1♥	2♠

There are many options, including to use them preemptively to show weak hands ('Weak Jump Shifts'). I'm sure you're really anxious to find out more about bidding with next to nothing but I'll deal with this later in the book in Step 20.

One treatment that I personally like is to use 1♠-3♥ to show an invitational hand with long hearts (you can still use 1♥-2♠ as a weak jump shift).

♠ 7 ♥ K Q 10 9 8 3 2 ♦ A 8 3 ♣ 7 2

On such a hand, you are really not interested in hearing partner suggest a new suit as trumps and will have little or no tolerance for spades. As much as possible, partner should focus on accepting or rejecting the game-try in hearts, or (on very rare occasions) consider playing in notrump.

Your only further obligations after the start 1♠-3♥ will be to respect partner's sign-off in whatever game he chooses or, if appropriate, co-operate in any slam suggestion.

2) The 3NT response

Partner	You		Partner	You
1♠	3NT		1♥	3NT

This is a very bulky and space-consuming response, and should therefore be assigned a very specific meaning. A little research will reveal several options, but I prefer to use it to show a balanced 15-17 HCP with 3-3-3-4 or 3-3-4-3 shape:

♠ Q 7 6 ♥ K J 5 ♦ A K 6 4 ♣ A 8 7

would be typical.

Partner's choice of rebids will be focused on:

- *Playing in his major or in notrump.*
- *Whether or not to move towards a slam.*
- *Rarely but occasionally suggesting a second suit as trumps.*

With most balanced or even semi-balanced hands, partner will choose to play in notrump since the partnership will have all suits stopped, the lead coming up to the strong hand and, assuming he has only a 5-card major for the opening, only an 8-card fit that might be susceptible to damage if a bad trump break exists. Since there will be no ruffs in the short hand, it is likely you will make at least as many tricks in notrump as in the major suit.

Summary

✓ After 1♥-1♠, opener rebids much the same as he would after a 1NT forcing response — remembering, of course, to raise spades if he can.

✓ After 1♥-1♠, opener's 1NT rebid shows a 12-14 HCP balanced hand but doesn't promise a stopper in all unbid suits.

✓ If you decide to play 1♠-3♥ to show an invitational hand with long hearts and no spade fit, opener should almost always focus on playing in hearts.

✓ After a response of 3NT to an opening 1♥ or 1♠, opener should be well placed to guide the partnership towards proper level and/or strain because of the very specific requirements (15-17 HCP in a balanced hand) for the 3NT response.

OTHER AUCTIONS STARTING 1♥ OR 1♠

NOW TRY THESE...

1
- ♠ A 7
- ♥ K J 9 5 4
- ♦ J 7 6
- ♣ K 8 7

You	Partner
1♥	1♠
?	

2
- ♠ A Q 4
- ♥ K Q 9 7 5
- ♦ J 8 7
- ♣ 9 5

You	Partner
1♥	1♠
?	

3
- ♠ Q 3
- ♥ A K Q 10 9 4
- ♦ A J 7
- ♣ K 8

You	Partner
1♥	1♠
?	

4
- ♠ A Q 6 5
- ♥ K Q J 8 7
- ♦ A 5
- ♣ K 7

You	Partner
1♥	1♠
?	

5
- ♠ K 8
- ♥ A Q 9 7 6
- ♦ K J 8
- ♣ A J 8

You	Partner
1♥	1♠
?	

6
- ♠ 7
- ♥ A Q J 8 7 6
- ♦ A K 8
- ♣ Q 8 7

You	Partner
1♥	1♠
?	

7
- ♠ A 8 7 6 3 2
- ♥ 8 5
- ♦ A K 8
- ♣ K 8

You	Partner
1♠	3♥[1]
?	

1. Invitational, long hearts.

8
- ♠ A K Q 8 7
- ♥ K 8 7
- ♦ A 9 6 4
- ♣ 9

You	Partner
1♠	3♥[1]
?	

1. Invitational, long hearts.

9
- ♠ A Q 6 5 4
- ♥ K J 8 7
- ♦ A Q
- ♣ 7 6

You	Partner
1♠	3NT
?	

10
- ♠ A Q 6 5 4
- ♥ K Q 8 7 3
- ♥ J 7
- ♣ 8

You	Partner
1♠	3NT
?	

ANSWERS

1 1NT You have 12-14 HCP and a balanced hand – what's a diamond stopper among friends?

2 2♠ The best alternative of a bad lot as 2♥ should show six cards and 1NT would lead partner to expect a stopper in at least one of the minors. Besides, your partner plays the hands so well that raising on three trumps should be routine!

3 3NT The 'source of tricks' rebid to show 6+ cards in a nearly solid heart suit with 17-19 HCP and outside stoppers – perfect!

4 4♠ You have 4-card support plus 18-20 HCP with no side suit shortness.

5 2NT This shows 18-19 HCP and a balanced hand.

6 3♥ This is natural with 6+ cards in the suit plus a medium hand – invitational with 16-18 HCP.

7 4♥ Don't let your spade length distract you. The heart fit is proven and you have enough strength for game but it's unlikely that you can fill enough holes for anything but a very lucky slam.

8 4NT The fit looks to be awesome – you have first-round control in two suits, second-round control in the fourth suit and a source of tricks in spades. All that remains to be seen is whether you have enough aces to underwrite a slam.

9 4NT This is a quantitative notrump raise – you can't have better than a 4-3 heart fit and you know the spade fit is only 5-3. In addition, you won't be able to ruff anything in partner's hand. So notrump will likely be at least as good as a suit contract – go ahead and invite slam.

10 4♥ You want to offer partner a choice of majors.

S T E P

THE LIGHT FANTASTIC

♥ Have you heard or read of a logical reason why you should place your partner with a weaker hand than the two adversaries because all three have passed? *Criticus.* **Contract Simplicitas.** *1933.*

Many players think the practice of opening with shaded values in third or fourth seat is a somewhat disreputable tendency best left to the club sharpies. Not so! There are sound tactical reasons for slightly lowering your requirements for opening the bidding with one of a major after two or three passes.

Among those reasons:

* *The deal may still belong to your side* in partscore (or even game) even though you have a hand you wouldn't have opened in first or second seat. (This is particularly true if you're following the guidelines for opening bid requirements in first or second seat that we discussed in Step 2.)

* *You may be able to suggest a good lead* to your partner in case the opponents buy the contract.

* *You may disrupt the opponents' bidding*, causing them to arrive in the wrong contract.

How low do we go in third seat?

Obviously, a hand that was worth opening 1♥ or 1♠ in first or second seat should also be worth opening in third or fourth (more about this later) but the 'light' opening bid may be made with slightly different third or fourth seat criteria.

For a light third seat opening, you might go as low as 10 HCP as long as the suit you're bidding is respectable (similar to overcall quality — i.e. a suit you want led) and the hand has 1½ defensive tricks. In addition, we might relax the requirement that 1♥ or 1♠ guarantees a five-card suit and bid a four-card suit of good quality.

So, after two passes, 1♥ is fine with

♠ A4 ♥ K Q J 10 5 ♦ 9 7 6 ♣ 6 5 3

as the suit is excellent and the hand does have 1½ defensive tricks. Even with

♠ A K J 4 ♥ K 8 7 ♦ 7 6 5 ♣ 9 5 4

you should open 1♠ — it's a great suit, which is only short one card in spades, and your bid is only 1 HCP away from being the truth. But with

♠ J 6 5 4 3 ♥ K 7 6 ♦ A Q 4 ♣ 4 3

pass is better as the suit is very poor. With

♠ 6 4 ♥ K Q J 10 ♦ J 9 7 6 ♣ A 5 3

opening 1♥ is acceptable as the suit is very good and the hand has 1½ defensive tricks.

Is it different in fourth seat?

When considering whether to open light in fourth seat, keep in mind two new considerations;

- *If you pass, the bidding is over and at least you haven't incurred a minus score. In other words, if you're considering opening light, your target is a plus score. Seems obvious, doesn't it?*

- *At least for the time being, there are no opponents to disrupt the bidding.*

When you're in fourth seat with 9-11 HCP, it's very likely each of the other players also has about 9-11 HCP. In these instances, the key to winning the auction will frequently be ownership of the spade suit. The side with a spade fit can always outbid their opponents without having to go to a new level. A guideline you can use to help you decide whether to open light in fourth seat is called 'Cansino Count', named after British expert Jonathan Cansino. Applying this yardstick, you add up your HCP and then add 1 point for every spade you hold.

If the answer comes to at least 15 Cansino Count points, you should (could) open.

So, after three passes, with

♠ A Q J 6 5 ♥ K 10 5 4 ♦ 6 ♣ 8 7 3

open 1♠ (you have a 15 Cansino Count), but with

♠ 7 ♥ K J 10 5 4 ♦ A Q 3 ♣ J 4 3 2

you are better advised to pass (only 12 Cansino Count points) as the opponents likely own the spade suit. You would open this hand in third seat however — good suit, some defense.

What changes after a third or fourth seat opening?

Before you get too terrified about these opening bids with sub-minimum values, rest assured that we will be making some accommodations for them in our bidding structure. But whatever you do, don't develop 'light opening paranoia' — don't be afraid to bid as responder because your partner might have opened with a dog of a hand.

The main thing that will have changed after a third or fourth seat opening is so obvious that it's something that a lot of players overlook. *When responder is a passed hand, he doesn't have the values for an opening bid!* Thus any and all responses he might want to make will be with hands in the 0-11 HCP range — he can't have any more!

In very simple terms, a passed-hand responder cannot have enough to force to game, so the most he will be able to do in the majority of bidding situations is invite to game (of course, there are still times when responder will go directly to game based on a distributional fit).

Since the strong Two-over-One and Forcing 1NT responses were all about separating responder's game-forcing hands from his game-invitational hands, significant changes will occur in our responding structure — and that's what the next Step is all about.

Summary

✓ A third seat 1♥ or 1♠ opening may be made with shaded values as long as the suit is decent and the hand has 1½ defensive tricks. The suit itself may be only four cards long.

✓ A light fourth seat opening should only be contemplated if the hand has at least 15 Cansino Count points.

✓ A passed-hand responder cannot make forcing-to-game responses since he can't have opening bid values.

THE LIGHT FANTASTIC

NOW TRY THESE...

On each of the following hands (a) What is your call after two passes to you? (b) What is your call after three passes to you?

1. ♠ A Q 10 6 5 4
    ♥ A 4 3
    ♦ 7
    ♣ 9 5 4

2. ♠ K Q 3
    ♥ A J 10 5 4 3
    ♦ 6
    ♣ 10 4 3

3. ♠ 6
    ♥ A Q J 6
    ♦ A Q 10 5 4
    ♣ 7 6 5

4. ♠ A 10 6 5
    ♥ K Q J 5
    ♦ Q 3
    ♣ 9 6 5

5. ♠ K Q J 10 2
    ♥ 7
    ♦ 8 7 5 4
    ♣ K J 6

6. ♠ 4 2
    ♥ K Q J 6 4 3
    ♦ K 5 4
    ♣ 10 6

ANSWERS

1 a) 1♠ Good suit, some defensive strength.

    b) 1♠ Same but some partnerships like a 4th seat 2♠ bid with this type of hand — it's largely a matter of style, a maximum two-bid or a minimum one-bid.

2 a) 1♥ Good suit, perhaps more defensive strength than a weak two-bid.

    b) Pass Not enough Cansino Count points (only 13) for a 4th seat one-bid but if you can't bear to pass you might try 2♥ as you do have some defensive strength versus spades if the opponents come back to life.

3 1♦ In both seats this is a 1♦ opening just the same as it would be in first or second seat.

4 1♥ In both seats, this is the type of hand you should open 1♥. As you'll see in the next Step, nothing bad will usually happen and two positive things might: If the opponents buy the hand, you would greatly prefer a heart lead to a club (your alternative suit for an opening bid) and second, your future with this hand in an offensive sense is in the majors and the heart opening makes immediate headway towards finding a major-suit fit.

5 1♠ A toughie in both situations as either Pass, 1♠ or 2♠ could work out best. However, I don't like to be passive with spades and as you'll see, a lot of good things could happen after 1♠, so that would be my choice.

6 a) 2♥ A classic weak two-bid.

    b) Pass Don't preempt in fourth seat — especially without spades.

AFTER A 3RD OR
4TH SEAT 1♥ OR 1♠

> ♥ Be an optimist in play and a pessimist in declaration. ***Criticus.***
> **Contract Simplicitas.** *1933*

The main thing to keep in mind when replying to a third or fourth seat opening is that you are a passed hand! While obvious, this means that you will not have enough values to want to force to game opposite a possible minimum (not to mention sub-minimum) opening bid. Accordingly, you can if you wish modify the meanings for your responses to accommodate both the range of values you will hold (0-11 HCP) and the possibility that partner might be, on occasion, 'light'.

As much as possible, you still want to be able to distinguish varying degrees of support for partner's major, particularly when game and/or slam is in view. The higher level contracts will usually be possible when you are at the upper end of your possible strength, i.e. 9-11 HCP.

There are a number of ways you can approach these 'passed hand' auctions, depending on how simple or complicated you want to make your life.

The simple approach

The easiest (although not necessarily the best) way to deal with the situation is not to change anything – treat the auction exactly as you do when responder is not a passed hand. Since you will never have a hand where you want to force to game, your Two-over-One responses will simply be eliminated from the structure. You'll still use a Forcing 1NT, Bergen raises, and everything else we've talked about.

Yes, it's easy to remember but it doesn't make best use of your opportunities. I recommend going for something a bit more complex.

Adding a little complexity

A very useful gadget that you can add here is a convention called Drury, which in its basic form uses the 2♣ response by a passed hand to show maximum values with a fit for opener's major – basically a limit raise. The simplest form of the convention (actually technically called Reverse Drury) is described in detail in Seagram and Smith's *25 Bridge Conventions You Should Know*, among other places. There are several more complex versions of Drury, but you should start with the simple one and progress from there when you feel you're ready.

If you do add Drury, you may also want to use the other two-over-one responses (2♦ and 2♥) as natural bids to show a hand with a good suit and 10-12 HCP, so that in this auction

You	Oppt.	Partner	Oppt.
pass	pass	1♠	pass
?			

you would bid 2♦ with something like

♠ 5   ♥ Q 4 3 2   ♦ A Q 10 5 4   ♣ K 8 7

For the really ambitious

One of the most significant changes you can make with passed-hand status will be the modification of a 1NT response from 'forcing for one round' to 'semi-forcing'. The 'semi' part of the name means that partner does not need to rebid with a balanced minimum (a bad 13 HCP or less) since there is very little possibility of a sensible game contract when he has this hand type and you have a non-fitting 11 HCP or less without (as we'll see) a very good long suit of your own. The biggest difference in the types of hands that might respond 1NT is that none of them will contain support (two little cards as a maximum) for partner's major.

This goes very well with the Drury convention, and allows you if you wish to drop some of the Bergen raise structure. This leaves the single raise of partner's major to be used for supporting hands (3- or 4-card support) in the 5-9 HCP range. Remember, as a passed hand you can't bid 1NT with the weak raise type of hand because the 1NT response is no longer forcing and you may well languish in 1NT when the major-suit fit would be superior. In fact, all supporting hands will either use Drury or make an immediate raise.

What happens after all that…?

Assuming that you decide to add Drury and a semi-forcing 1NT to your passed-hand auctions, how will the auction continue?

1) After a raise

Nothing much changes for opener, except after a passed-hand's single raise. Now as opener you need to be just a little bit careful because partner may have a weak raise hand type like

♠ Q65 ♥ K6 ♦ 87632 ♣ 1087

(a minimum passed-hand raise of 1♠ to 2♠).

You should pass with a minimum hand, usually less than 16 HCP with no great distributional assets. You can try for game via the by-now familiar HSGT approach when you're in the 16-18 HCP range or go directly to game when stronger. On rare occasions, you will be so strong that you will want to explore slam potential via a 'false HSGT' and see what reaction you get, bidding on to at least game in any event.

2) After a semi-forcing 1NT response

The 'semi' part of the description means that as opener you should rebid exactly the same way you would have opposite an unpassed hand except that you should pass whenever you hold a balanced minimum – a bad 13 HCP or less (the hands when you would have made that awkward 3-card minor rebid). In other words, any rebid will show either extra HCP or unbalanced distribution.

3) Drury auctions

These will be the biggest adjustment you will have to make for passed-hand auctions after major openings, but they combine significant accuracy (when opener has a good hand) with safety (when opener might have taken some liberties in opening in the first place).

BY THE WAY

If you decide to drop the Bergen-style raises as a passed hand, you can use the 3♣ and 3♦ bids to show a maximum passed-hand with a good 6-card (sometimes 7-card) suit. One benefit of this approach is that you won't feel you should stretch to open such a hand in first or second seat since you can describe it later. An alternative meaning is the 'fit-showing jump'. This shows a maximum passed hand with nine cards between the suit bid and partner's major. This approach is popular, but the hands for it don't come up as often as for the first alternative.

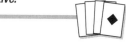

You show a lack of game interest by bidding two of your agreed major and partner should subside. Remember you have license to open with hands that you wouldn't open in first or second seat and the Drury response and signoff rebid is the partnership's protection mechanism.

Frequently, you will simply want to be in game opposite a limit raise, knowing that a slam would need more than a passed hand can deliver. In those cases, you should just bid game.

There are many ways to play other rebids by opener, all of which are made on hands that envisage at least a possibility of either game or slam. When you are familiar with the basic convention, you should discuss these sequences with your partner and decide how you want to play them. In the simplest version of Drury, the conventional rebid of 2♦ simply says you don't want to sign off yet. Partner can then show a maximum limit raise by jumping to three of the major, or simply bid two of the major with a lesser hand.

Summary

When responding to partner's third- or fourth-seat major seat opening you can:

- ✓ Use exactly the same system with no changes.

- ✓ Use the Drury 2♣ convention to show a limit raise.

- ✓ Treat the 1NT response as only semi-forcing.

AFTER A 3RD OR 4TH SEAT 1♥ OR 1♠

NOW TRY THESE...

You've passed in first seat with each of the following hands and partner has opened 1♠ in third seat. What is your response?

1	♠ Q 4 ♥ K J 8 7 ♦ Q 9 8 7 ♣ Q 7 3	**2**	♠ 5 ♥ K 8 7 ♦ J 7 4 ♣ A Q 10 9 4 3
3	♠ Q J 7 6 ♥ K J 7 ♦ 7 6 5 ♣ 5 4 3	**4**	♠ J 6 4 2 ♥ 6 5 ♦ A 8 7 ♣ J 10 9 8
5	♠ A 10 7 6 5 ♥ 6 5 4 ♦ K Q 4 2 ♣ 7		

6-10 Now go back to the five examples above and respond again, assuming your partner's opening bid was 1♥ in third seat.

You've opened 1♠ in third seat with each of the following hands. What is your rebid opposite the indicated response?

♠ K J 7 6 5 ♥ A 7 ♦ Q 7 6 ♣ K 8 7	**11** **12** **13**	1NT 2♣ 2♦
♠ K J 10 4 3 ♥ A J 6 3 ♦ A ♣ 8 7 3	**14** **15** **16**	1NT 2♣ 2♦
♠ A K J 10 5 2 ♥ K J 7 ♦ A 4 ♣ 9 2	**17** **18** **19**	1NT 2♣ 2♦

ANSWERS

1	1NT	The same bid you would make as an unpassed hand.
2	3♣	Good 6-card suit and a maximum passed hand.
3	2♠	This single raise now shows either 3- or 4-card support.
4	2♠	This single raise now shows either 3- or 4-card support.
5	4♠	Direct game raise just as if you weren't a passed hand. The scientists (chickens?) among you might be content with 2♣ Drury. The problem usually arises when opener signs off at 2♠ over this and you feel you've got too much not to make one more try so you re-raise and leave the last mistake to partner! I prefer the less nerve-wracking approach of the direct game raise and saving more time and energy for the play.
6	2♣	Drury.
7	2♣	Drury. There's no convenient way to show your clubs anyway.
8	2♥	You've found a heart fit so forget about the spades!
9	1♠	Sometimes life is simple.
10	2♣	Drury. Yes, on occasion opener might have opened with a minimum with both majors (♠KQJ5 ♥AJ1053 ♦87 ♣92) and you will miss a superior spade fit. However, a 1♠ response would be non-forcing and you may get to play right there without having divulged your heart fit. Also, when opener has a good hand your heart support will be almost impossible to show after the 1♠ response even when opener does rebid.
11	Pass	No need to make that 2♣ rebid any more.
12	2♦	The non-sign-off rebid over Drury. Game is unlikely, but not out of the question if partner has four trumps.
13	Pass	You'd like to bid 3♦ to keep the opponents quiet, but partner might get too excited. You won't make game opposite any hand partner didn't open.
14	2♥	Natural rebid with an unbalanced hand. Non-forcing.
15	2♦	The non-sign-off rebid over Drury. Game is quite likely, especially if partner has four trumps.
16	2♥	Natural rebid with an unbalanced hand. Non-forcing.
17	3♠	Natural and invitational.
18	4♠	Fit and values are enough for game but slam is very unlikely.
19	3♠	Natural and game-forcing now partner has shown 10+ HCP.

IN A MINOR KEY

♥ Opening is an overbid in that it announces that it will take more tricks than are possible with the cards held by the bidder. **The Official System of Contract Bridge.** *1931*

Strictly speaking, the only direct application of the Two-over-One system after a minor-suit opening will occur in the auction 1♦-2♣. This sequence is natural and 100% forcing to game, just like the Two-over-One responses to a major-suit opening bid by an unpassed hand. Since not all hands responding to 1♦ openings will qualify for this treatment and since inconsiderate partners will occasionally(!) open 1♣, we also need a philosophically consistent approach to those auctions – recognizing that they will be little different, if at all, from Standard methods. Let's examine the possibilities.

The only Two-over-One auction

Partner	You
1♦	2♣

You will make this bid on two types of hand:

1) ***Any hand strong enough to force to game where clubs is your longest suit and you have at least five of them.*** In terms of strength, you can have anything from a minimum opening bid up to and including enough for an old-fashioned Standard jump shift. Beware – this 2♣ response does not deny a 4-card (or longer) major suit. You might easily have a 4-card major if you also have five or more clubs; you might even have a 5-card major if you also have six or more clubs.

Any of the following hands would qualify, therefore:

♠ A J 6 5   ♥ 6   ♦ Q 5 4   ♣ A K 8 7 5

14 HCP – enough to force to game, and the clubs are longer than spades.

♠ A 4   ♥ 8 7 6   ♦ A Q   ♣ A K Q 8 7 6

19 HCP, clearly enough to force to game. As we'll see soon (Step 15) we're going to have another use for a jump shift (1♦-3♣) so 2♣ will frequently be bid over 1♦ on very strong hands.

♠ A K J 6 5   ♥ 5   ♦ 7   ♣ A Q J 7 6 5

Again, enough to force to game and your clubs are longer than your spades. Don't worry – spades are not going to get lost as a possible trump suit!

2) ***Some balanced hands without a 4-card major*** that don't fit either the stopper requirements or strength parameters for an immediate notrump response (more about this in Step 14). When you are balanced, you will usually have 12-14 HCP or 18+ HCP (with 15-17, as you'll see, you have a convenient notrump bid available). A couple of typical hands would be

♠ 8 7 6   ♥ 5 4 3   ♦ A 4 3   ♣ A K Q 4

Enough strength for a game-force and 2♣ is the natural start.

♠ K J 7   ♥ A J 6   ♦ Q 6 5   ♣ A K 5 4

A strong balanced hand with 18+ HCP, no 4-card major and fewer than five diamonds: start with a 2♣ response.

Other responses to 1♦

There are some differences in the other possible auctions depending on which minor is opened, so we're going to look at them separately. We're also going to ignore notrump responses for the time being; they will be dealt with in the next Step.

After a 1♦ opening, with 6+ HCP, if you're going to respond in a major, you will bid your longer suit first. With two equal-length major suits you should generally follow the 'up-the-line' Standard practice: with 4-4 in the majors, respond 1♥, with 5-5 respond 1♠ and bid hearts on the next round — in both cases, you should not be overly concerned with relative suit quality or your hand's total strength. (Keep in mind that you should reply 2♣ if you have game-forcing strength with at least five clubs even if you have a 4-card major).

Responses to 1♣

Even ignoring the notrump responses (again, that's the next Step) this is a more controversial subject, because some players like to ignore the diamond suit in the cause of exploring for a major-suit fit. This is more a style thing than anything else, and again, there's no right or wrong. Whatever you've been doing up to now is fine to continue. However, if you want to be up on modern theory, you should know that there are two fairly distinct schools of thought:

1) **The 'Walsh' approach.** With rare exceptions, responder always shows a 4-card major as a priority, frequently bypassing a diamond suit of equal or greater length.

2) **The classic Standard approach.** Responder always bids up the line and never bypasses a diamond suit so as to bid a 4-card major.

Both approaches have some merits and many adherents and I won't think less of you whichever method you decide to adopt – just make sure you're aware of the relative pitfalls of each. As befits a peaceable Canadian, my own preferred approach is somewhat of a compromise: I like to respond up the line after 1♣ except when I have a relatively weak hand that I consider worth only one bid and most of my strength is in my 4-card major suit. This is especially important when the major is hearts and you're short in spades as the opponents may be about to get into the auction and a possible heart fit might get lost in the stampede. Using this approach, here are some example hands:

Partner	You
1♣	1♦

♠ A J 7 6 ♥ 5 4 ♦ K 8 7 6 5 ♣ 5 2

No hurry to bypass diamonds, just bid your hand naturally.

Partner	You
1♣	1♦

♠ 6 5 ♥ A K Q 4 ♦ A 9 7 6 5 ♣ 6 5

If you were to bid hearts first and diamonds later, that would tend to show 5+ hearts.

Partner	You
1♣	1♦

♠ Q 4 3 2 ♥ 9 7 6 ♦ 5 4 3 2 ♣ A 5

Use the up the line approach with two 4-card suits.

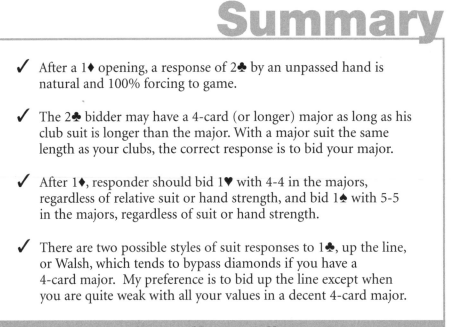

Partner	You
1♣	1♥

♠ 5 ♥ A Q J 6 ♦ 8 5 4 3 ♣ 9 5 3 2

Here's an example of bypassing diamonds to bid the major since it's 'where you live' – what values you do have are in hearts and your spade shortness suggests the opponents might soon be heard from, possibly preempting your side out of a heart fit. A diamond fit is less likely and less profitable if it does exist.

Partner	You
1♣	1♠

♠ A J 7 6 5 ♥ 4 3 ♦ K Q J 5 4 ♣ 5

Here you bid the higher ranking of two 5-card suits, as always.

Summary

- ✓ After a 1♦ opening, a response of 2♣ by an unpassed hand is natural and 100% forcing to game.

- ✓ The 2♣ bidder may have a 4-card (or longer) major as long as his club suit is longer than the major. With a major suit the same length as your clubs, the correct response is to bid your major.

- ✓ After 1♦, responder should bid 1♥ with 4-4 in the majors, regardless of relative suit or hand strength, and bid 1♠ with 5-5 in the majors, regardless of suit or hand strength.

- ✓ There are two possible styles of suit responses to 1♣, up the line, or Walsh, which tends to bypass diamonds if you have a 4-card major. My preference is to bid up the line except when you are quite weak with all your values in a decent 4-card major.

IN A MINOR KEY

NOW TRY THESE...

What is your next bid on each of the following hands?

1 ♠ J 7 6 5
   ♥ K 7
   ♦ J 8 5 4
   ♣ K 6 5

Partner	You
1♦	?

2 ♠ K Q 3 2
   ♥ Q 3
   ♦ 7 6
   ♣ A Q J 6 5

Partner	You
1♦	?

3 ♠ A 9 7 6 5
   ♥ K 10 9 5 3
   ♦ 6 5
   ♣ 6

Partner	You
1♦	?

4 ♠ Q 6 5 4
   ♥ 6 4
   ♦ A 9 7 6 4 3
   ♣ 6

Partner	You
1♦	?

5 ♠ A Q 4
   ♥ 8 7
   ♦ A 6 5 4
   ♣ K J 5 4

Partner	You
1♦	?

6 ♠ J 7 6 5
   ♥ K 7
   ♦ J 8 5 4
   ♣ K 6 5

Partner	You
1♣	?

7 ♠ K Q 3 2
   ♥ Q 3
   ♦ 7 6
   ♣ A Q J 6 5

Partner	You
1♣	?

8 ♠ A 9 7 6 5
   ♥ K 10 9 5 3
   ♦ 6 5
   ♣ 6

Partner	You
1♣	?

9 ♠ Q 6 5 4
   ♥ 6 4
   ♦ A 9 7 6 4 3
   ♣ 6

Partner	You
1♣	?

10 ♠ A Q 4
    ♥ 8 7
    ♦ A 6 5 4
    ♣ K J 5 4

Partner	You
1♣	?

ANSWERS

1	1♠	Natural up the line response.
2	2♣	Natural and game-forcing.
3	1♠	The right start with 5-5 in the majors.
4	1♠	The natural one-level response. This is your best shot to find the major-suit fit and you can fall back on showing support for partner at your next turn (assuming no spade fit is found).
5	2♣	Natural and game-forcing.
6	1♦	Also the natural response. In accord with "The Principle of Separation" that we've encountered previously, the more suits you skip over in reply to your partner's opening bid, especially at the one-level, the more likely you are to have 5 cards in the bid suit. Thus, don't be in a big hurry to bid 1♠ over 1♣ with only 4 so-so cards since, in a pinch, partner will sometimes assume you might have 5.
7	1♠	Show your 4-card major before you worry about raising clubs.
8	1♠	The right start with 5-5 in the majors.
9	1♦	As the spades are of unexceptional quality and the diamond suit is two cards longer, follow the up the line length-first approach.
10	1♦	Natural, up the line, hoping to hear partner bid hearts so you can seize your beloved notrump.

NOTRUMP RESPONSES
TO MINORS

♥ To play good bridge you must learn the fundamental formulae that comprise a bidding system and, this achieved, you must use your head. **The Official System of Contract Bridge.** *1931*.

There are no great differences here from what you have been used to playing in Standard. However, it's worth running over the structure again, if only for completeness. The two critical points regarding notrump responses to opening bids of 1♣ or 1♦ are these:

- *Any notrump response denies a 4-card or longer major suit.*

- *The 1NT response, in contrast to 1NT over a major-suit opening bid, is not forcing.* It is a limited bid that opener will only bid over with extra HCP and/or unbalanced distribution (Step 17).

Let's look at the three possible notrump bids after partner opens one of a minor.

The 1NT response

We can summarize this response as follows:

- *6-10 HCP*

- *No 4-card major*

- *No 5-card support for partner's minor*

- *Not forcing*

These are some typical hands for a 1NT response to 1♦:

Partner	You
1♦	1NT

♠ 6 5 4 ♥ 4 3 2 ♦ J 7 6 ♣ A K 4 3

♠ Q J 4 ♥ Q J 4 ♦ Q 4 ♣ Q 9 6 5 4

♠ K 8 7 ♥ 9 7 6 ♦ A Q 6 ♣ 9 7 6 5

Over 1♣, some people like to bid 1NT whenever they have a flattish hand in the right point range, tending to ignore a 4-card diamond suit. My advice is not to be in a big rush to bid 1NT over 1♣ with no values in one or both majors. You will usually be better off with a 1♦ response in such cases. These hands would qualify for a 1NT response over 1♣:

Partner	You
1♣	1NT

♠ Q 6 5 ♥ K 7 6 ♦ 9 7 5 4 ♣ A 4 3

♠ K J 7 ♥ Q 5 4 ♦ A 4 3 ♣ 9 8 5 4

However, on this hand

♠ 5 4 3 ♥ K J 4 ♦ A 6 5 4 ♣ 7 6 5

where you have nothing in spades, I would prefer to bid 1♦ instead.

Notice that when you respond 1NT to 1♣ you will usually have a balanced hand, while the same can't be said over a 1♦ opening. Quite often, you will have length in clubs but lack the strength for a game-forcing 2♣ response and have to reply 1NT by default.

♠ 5 4 3 ♥ 6 5 ♦ 8 2 ♣ A Q J 6 5 4

Here, for example, you have no major, no diamond support, and insufficient strength for 2♣, so it has to be 1NT over 1♦.

The 2NT response

This is not dissimilar to the 1NT response, except, of course, that it shows a better hand. Here are the basic requirements:

- *10-12 HCP*
- *no 4-card major*
- *no 5-card support for opener's minor*
- *invitational to game*
- *prefer to have all unbid suits stopped (but that is not always possible)*

You may be used to the now somewhat old-fashioned 13-15 HCP range for 2NT. It makes more sense to play this bid as invitational in a Two-over-One structure, since you'll have no problem creating a game force with the stronger hand (you'll always have a suit bid available, and often this will be a Two-over-One response which will force to game right away – then you can bid notrump on the next round).

Here are some example hands for this auction:

Partner	You
1♦	2NT

♠ K J 5   ♥ Q J 7   ♦ 5 4 3   ♣ A 7 6 5

11 HCP, no major = perfect!

♠ K 10 4   ♥ Q J 5   ♦ 3 2   ♣ A 10 9 8 3

A 'good' 10 HCP, balanced, invitational strength.

Notice that, just like the 1NT response to 1♦, the 2NT response over 1♦ will frequently include club length. Similarly:

Partner	You
1♣	2NT

♠ Q J 6   ♥ A 4   ♦ Q J 7 6   ♣ J 8 7 6

11 HCP, balanced, something in all unbid suits.

♠ Q 4 3   ♥ Q 9 7   ♦ Q 8 7   ♣ A 6 3 2

A so-so 10 HCP but you play notrump so well! 1NT would not be wrong on this hand if you are feeling pessimistic.

♠ K J 6   ♥ K 10 7   ♦ 8 7 4 3   ♣ A 10 5

11 HCP, balanced, almost a diamond stopper! You could also start with 1♦ on this hand if you wanted to.

The 3NT response

Since this is a very bulky, space-consuming response, it is critical to use it with care and with very narrow parameters so that you reach the best game contract and also so that you don't miss decent slams based on extra tricks developed from long suits.

Thus, the 3NT response shows:

- *15-17 HCP*
- *no 4-card major*
- *no 5-card support for partner's minor*
- *no good quality 5-card holding in the 'other' minor.* ('Good' in this context we usually take to mean K10xxx or better.)
- *all unbid suits stopped*

So after 1♣, bid 3NT with

♠ A Q 3   ♥ K Q 5   ♦ A J 6   ♣ 8 7 6 5

when you have 16 HCP, balanced, and all unbid suits stopped, but not with

♠ A Q 3   ♥ J 7 6   ♦ A K Q 5   ♣ J 7 6

where hearts are unstopped (prefer 1♦ instead on this hand). You should also not bid 3NT with

♠ K J 7   ♥ A 3   ♦ K Q 9   ♣ Q J 7 6 5

because you have 5-card support for partner's clubs (see Step 15).

After 1♦, bid 3NT with:

♠ K J 3   ♥ A 3   ♦ J 8 7 6   ♣ A K 7 6

(again 16 HCP, balanced, all unbid suits stopped) or with

♠ A Q 9   ♥ K J 8   ♦ A 6   ♣ Q 8 7 6 4

since your club suit is not good enough for a game-forcing 2♣ bid. However, with

♠ A J 6   ♥ K J 7   ♦ 8 7   ♣ A K J 8 7

2♣ is correct, even though you meet all the other criteria for a 3NT call. Finally, with

♠ A Q 4 3   ♥ K Q 4   ♦ Q 4   ♣ A 10 8 7

you have a 4-card major. The correct response to 1♣ or 1♦ is 1♠!

Summary

✓ All notrump responses to minor suit openings deny a 4-card or longer major suit.

✓ 1NT shows 6-10 HCP and is not forcing.

✓ 2NT shows 10-12 HCP and invites game. Ideally, all unbid suits will be stopped, but (sadly) this is not guaranteed.

✓ 3NT shows 15-17 HCP in a balanced hand with all unbid suits stopped and no great 'source of tricks' minor suit.

✓ 2NT and 3NT deny 5-card support for partner's minor.

NOTRUMP RESPONSES TO MINORS

NOW TRY THESE...

What is your response if partner opens 1♦?

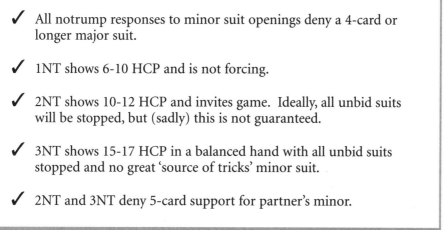

1	♠ Q J 7	2	♠ Q 4 3 2	3	♠ 4 3 2
	♥ K 10 8		♥ Q J 7		♥ 8 7 4
	♦ 7 6		♦ 7 6		♦ 9 6 3
	♣ A 10 9 8 5		♣ A Q 4 3		♣ A K 9 5
4	♠ Q J 10 5	5	♠ 4 3 2	6	♠ Q 3 2
	♥ K 7 6		♥ 9 8 7		♥ K 8 7
	♦ 7		♦ A Q J 9		♦ J 8 7
	♣ A K 8 7 6		♣ 6 5 2		♣ A 5 4 3

What is your response if partner opens 1♣?

7	♠ Q J 8	8	♠ K J 7	9	♠ K J 7
	♥ 8 5 3		♥ A 5 4		♥ A 4 3
	♦ A Q J 7		♦ A K Q 3 2		♦ K Q J 8
	♣ J 8 7		♣ 7 2		♣ Q J 6
10	♠ K J 7	11	♠ Q 10 8	12	♠ K Q 3
	♥ 10 6 5 4		♥ K J 8		♥ Q 6 5
	♦ A 5 4		♦ Q J 7 6		♦ 9 8 7 4
	♣ 7 4 2		♣ K 8 7		♣ J 10 8

ANSWERS

1   2NT   A 'good' 10 HCP, with something in all the unbid suits.

2   1♠   Of course! Just trying to trick you again!

3   1NT   Nothing else fits and you have to bid something with 7 HCP.

4   2♣   Natural and game-forcing.

5   2♦   A bit of a preview for Step 15 but even with only 4-card support for partner's possible 3-card minor, this bid shows 'where you live'.

6   1NT   A bad 10 HCP and nothing to bid at the one-level. Contrast with Question 1 above.

7   1♦   Nothing in hearts so don't strain to bid notrump when a convenient and reasonable alternative exists.

8   1♦   Right HCP for 3NT but your long suit is too good – a 'source of tricks'.

9   3NT   Bang on – 17 HCP, balanced, all unbid suits stopped.

10   1♥   Don't ignore that major!

11   2NT   An 'ugly' 12 HCP but something in every suit and remember that the bid is only invitational, plus your hand at least looks 'notrump-ish'.

12   1NT   Finish this section off with an easy one!

RAISING PARTNER'S MINOR

> ♥ The first round is the game-bidding round. *Criticus*. **Contract Simplicitas.** *1933.*

While admittedly they are not frequent, there will be occasions when you'll have good support for the minor suit partner opened and, in lieu of having anything better to bid, will want to show that support immediately. Since you know by now that your first responsibility as responder is to explore for a major suit fit, hands that call for an immediate minor-suit raise will not contain a 4-card major. Further, since a 1♣ or 1♦ opening bid will often be made on a 3-card suit, your immediate raises should all contain five or more cards in support (we'll see only one very rare exception to this general rule).

As a consumer of bidding ideas and systems, you will find a variety of schemes of minor-suit raises on the market. To choose an effective approach, you should look for a model that includes ways to raise a minor with weak, invitational and game-forcing hands. Perhaps you're already playing one you're comfortable with, in which case, be my guest — move right on to the next Step. However, if you are still in the market, you're in luck — we have a great model on display in our showroom — right this way!

The single raise

Partner	You	Partner	You
1♣	2♣	1♦	2♦

You were probably brought up with this one when you learned Standard, and it hasn't changed. A single raise shows:

- *6-9 HCP*

- *usually at least 5-card support*

- *no 4-card or longer major suit*

So, you raise 1♣ to 2♣ with these hands:

♠ Q4 ♥ 65 ♦ QJ76 ♣ K9876

♠ A43 ♥ 6 ♦ J876 ♣ QJ654

but not with:

♠ 5 ♥ 8743 ♦ K87 ♣ QJ654

(bid that major!) nor with

♠ AQ4 ♥ K87 ♦ 876 ♣ 10982

(you have only four clubs and 1NT is a better alternative).

There is, of course, an exception, which comes up very rarely — you will be well advised to raise the minor with 4-card support if that's where your hand's entire values lie, i.e. 'where you live'. So, raise 1♦ to 2♦ with

♠ 543 ♥ 54 ♦ AQJ6 ♣ 9765

and raise 1♣ to 2♣ with

♠ 543 ♥ 874 ♦ 432 ♣ AK65

Please, no 'short club' paranoia — it's only the two-level!

The limit raise

Partner	You	Partner	You
1♣	3♣	1♦	3♦

Depending on how long ago you learned your Standard, this too may have been part of it. You make an invitational 'limit raise' by raising partner's minor to the three-level with

- *10-12 HCP*

- *at least 5-card support*

- *no 4-card or longer major*

This is called a 'limit raise' since you will have reached the limit of your combined assets at the three-level unless partner has extra values (in HCP or distributional features) beyond a minimum opening bid.

So, after 1♣ raise to 3♣ with these hands:

♠ A4 ♥ 87 ♦ 10 4 3 2 ♣ K Q J 7 6

♠ 5 ♥ Q J 7 ♦ J 7 6 5 ♣ A Q J 7 6

but not with:

♠ A 7 6 5 ♥ 7 6 ♦ 5 4 ♣ A Q J 7 6

(bid that major!) nor with:

♠ 5 4 ♥ 7 6 3 ♦ A Q 10 3 ♣ K J 8 7

(you have only four clubs, so respond 1♦) nor on:

♠ J 10 6 ♥ Q J 6 ♦ A 4 3 ♣ K J 10 7

Here 2 NT is much more descriptive since you have only four clubs.

Game-forcing raises of opener's minor

Being able to tell partner immediately that you have a hand worth forcing to game, with serious minor-suit support, can be a decided plus. True to system philosophy, you create a game-force early on. Now you have time and room not only to reach the right game but also to find good minor-suit slams, a decided failing on the part of many systems.

As always in Two-over-One, you really don't need the old-fashioned jump shift in its classic sense of a natural response, forcing to game and inviting slam. Accordingly, it makes sense to co-opt the jump shift in the unbid minor to show a game-forcing raise of opener's minor. These bids are artificial and completely forcing to game. They are referred to as 'Criss-Cross minor-suit forcing raises' since a club response shows diamonds and vice versa.

Partner	You	Partner	You
1♣	2♦	1♦	3♣

These bids promise:

- *12+ HCP*
- *no 4-card or longer major*
- *at least 5-card support for opener's minor*

So, after partner opens 1♣, respond 2♦ with these hands:

♠ A 3 ♥ 7 6 ♦ K J 7 6 ♣ A Q 6 5 4

♠ A 4 3 ♥ Q 4 ♦ K 6 ♣ K Q J 7 6 5

♠ Q 4 3 ♥ A 4 ♦ K Q 5 ♣ A Q 10 5 4

However, with

♠ A4 ♥ K876 ♦ A3 ♣ AJ765

bid 1♥ — show your major first. Similarly, with

♠ KQJ ♥ 65 ♦ KQJ7 ♣ AQJ8

bid 1♦. You have only four clubs, and cannot bid notrump without a heart stopper.

Summary

✓ All immediate raises of opener's minor suit deny a 4-card or longer major suit.

✓ A single raise shows 6-9 HCP and almost always at least 5-card support.

✓ A double raise is a limit raise, inviting game, with 10-12 HCP and at least 5-card support.

✓ The Criss-Cross minor-suit jump shift responses (1♣-2♦ and 1♦-3♣) show a game-forcing raise of opener's minor with at least 5-card support and 12+ HCP.

✓ You can also play that a jump to the 3-level in a new suit (but not 1♦-3♣) is a 'splinter raise' with 12+ HCP, at least 5-card support for opener's minor and shortness in the bid suit. If you play this, your Criss-Cross bids deny side-suit shortness.

RAISING PARTNER'S MINOR

NOW TRY THESE...

What is your next bid on each of these hands?

1
♠ A Q 3 2
♥ 7
♦ K J 7 6
♣ J 8 7 6

Partner	You
1♣	?

2
♠ K 7 6
♥ K 8
♦ Q 4 3
♣ 9 7 6 4 3

Partner	You
1♣	?

3
♠ 6
♥ Q 3 2
♦ A J 7 6
♣ K J 8 7 6

Partner	You
1♣	?

4
♠ Q 4 3
♥ A 3
♦ Q 4 3
♣ K 9 8 5 4

Partner	You
1♣	?

5
♠ A 4
♥ 8
♦ A Q J 7
♣ K 9 7 6 4 3

Partner	You
1♣	?

6
♠ A J 6
♥ Q 4 3
♦ Q J 7 6
♣ J 10 7

Partner	You
1♦	?

7
♠ 6
♥ A 4
♦ A 10 8 7 4
♣ K Q J 7 6

Partner	You
1♦	?

8
♠ J 8 7 4
♥ 10 5
♦ A Q J 10 9
♣ 9 2

Partner	You
1♦	?

9
♠ A J 7
♥ K 10 4
♦ A Q 3 2
♣ K 8 7

Partner	You
1♦	?

10
♠ 7 6 4
♥ 9 5 2
♦ A Q 9 4
♣ 7 6 4

Partner	You
1♦	?

ANSWERS

1	1♦	Up the line of course!
2	2♣	Show that support! Don't be in too much of a hurry to 'grab the notrump' — supporting partner creates a firm foundation for further bidding — maybe!
3	3♣	A sensible limit raise with 5-card support and 11 HCP.
4	3♣	Again.
5	3♥	A splinter raise of partner's clubs.
6	2NT	Almost all suits stopped and certainly the most descriptive bid.
7	2♣	At first glance, you might bid 3♣ as a Criss-Cross artificial forcing raise or 3♠ as a splinter raise but, just as with our major-suit raises, immediate minor-suit raises should not usually have a great 'source of tricks' on the side, especially if there's a convenient natural alternative — which a response of 2♣ certainly offers in this case.
8	1♠	Bid that major!
9	3NT	To show 15-17 HCP without 5-card diamond support and all unbid suits stopped.
10	2♦	If you're too embarrassed to raise with only 4-card support (you really shouldn't be) put a heart in with your diamonds and complain about the lighting if you become dummy.

STEP

REBIDS AFTER
MINOR-SUIT OPENINGS

♥ Each player should bid only his own cards, allowing his partner to bid his. **Dudley Courtenay. The System the Experts Play. *1934.***

As always, opener's rebids will depend to some extent on the response to his opening bid. As you'll see, the auctions we want to spend the most time on are those that start with a Two-over-One response.

Do the One-over-One auctions change?

When responder makes a One-over-One response to a 1♣ or 1♦ opening bid, he is promising 6+ HCP and at least four cards in the suit he bids. This response is forcing for one round only and the hunt for the right strain and level is on! There is nothing here that need be any different from what you are currently playing as Standard, so I'm not going waste your time and my space by going through it all again for you (there's a quick summary at the end of this Step if you need it). However, there are some small warnings that bear repeating:

1) Up the line principles at the one-level apply to both partners. If a player 'skips over' a possible suit, especially a major suit, he is assumed to have fewer than four cards in that suit. For example:

You	Partner
1♣	1♦
1♠	

In this auction, you do not have four hearts.

2) When a major-suit fit (at least eight cards between the two hands) has been found, the player who first realizes it should immediately let his partner in on the good news. Support with support.

♠ A Q J 6 ♥ 8 5 4 3 ♦ 5 4 ♣ A K 7

You	Partner
1♣	1♥
?	

I know it's tempting here to decide that your hearts are fairly poor and your spades are oh, so much better and rebid 1♠. But you will never be able to convince partner that you have a 4-4 heart fit if you don't raise right away!

3) There's another common complaint we really need to deal with here. 'But partner will think I've got a short club if I don't rebid my 5-card club suit.' Answer: 'Short clubs' are for diminutive golfers! Things will work out, trust me, if you get rid of this minor-suit paranoia and try to avoid rebidding your minor without at least six of them. If your 5-card minor will make a sensible trump suit, partner will usually be able to volunteer support later.

4) There are some players ('notrump hogs') who think it's okay to rebid 1NT or 2NT with a singleton — sometimes even with a void(!) — in partner's suit. I believe you really should try to avoid doing this; it makes the auction very difficult if you tell partner you're balanced and then try to change the message later on. Typically this comes up when you open 1♣ with something like

♠ 6 ♥ A Q 3 2 ♦ K 7 6 ♣ A 10 7 6 5

and partner is inconsiderate enough to respond 1♠. Yes, you lack the strength to reverse into 2♥, but rather than rebid 1NT and promise a balanced hand I would recommend you rebid 2♣ and make the lesser-of-evils lie about your club length.

By the time opener has made his rebid, in a great many situations, responder will have a fairly clear idea either the right strain or the right level, and often both. There are, however, some situations where responder will need to be able to keep the auction open and get more information from opener. We'll be looking at ways to handle these auctions in Step 18 (Fourth Suit Forcing), Step 21 (New Minor Forcing) and Step 22 (Bidding after a Reverse).

The Two-over-One auction

You	Partner
1♦	2♣
?	

As the only Two-over-One sequence after a minor suit opening bid, this particular start poses some unique problems:

- *Since it's usually easier to take nine tricks than eleven, you're probably going to want to end up in 3NT more often than not. However, you will have to make sure that you have stoppers in the major suits.*

- *A minor suit game and/or slam may still be a possibility so you have to make allowances for exploration in that direction as well.*

By now you'll be used to my telling you that there are many ways to play these sequences, and it is certainly true of this auction. What I'm going to describe is a straightforward rebid structure that probably isn't very different from what you're already playing.

1) Rebidding 2NT

You	Partner
1♦	2♣
2NT	

Usually 12-14 HCP in a balanced hand, preferably with stoppers in both majors, but this won't always be possible or totally practical if the hand doesn't fit any of the other alternatives you're about to encounter. However, you will also make this rebid with 18-19 HCP in a balanced hand with all unbid suits stopped (remember, the 2♣ response is forcing to game so you will get a further opportunity to clarify whether you have the usual minimum or the extra-strength hand). So rebid 2NT on either of these hands:

♠ A J 7　♥ Q 4 2　♦ A J 5 4 2　♣ 6 5

♠ A Q J 7　♥ Q J 4　♦ A K J 5　♣ 6 5

2) Rebidding 2♦

You	Partner
1♦	2♣
2♦	

Real diamonds! At least five cards in length, generally a minimum hand. May have a stopper in one but rarely both majors (unless unbalanced, when you will usually have at least six diamonds). A typical hand would be

♠ A 8 7　♥ 5　♦ A K J 5 4 2　♣ Q 4 3

3) Rebidding 3♦

You	Partner
1♦	2♣
3♦	

Extra values (15+ HCP) plus extra diamonds (at least six) in a generally unbalanced hand but not a hand that would qualify for a 3NT rebid (see below).

♠ A Q 7 ♥ 5 ♦ A K J 10 4 2 ♣ Q 4 3

4) Rebidding 2♥ or 2♠

You	Partner	You	Partner
1♦	2♣	1♦	2♣
2♥		2♠	

These are reverses, usually with four cards in the major bid and always with longer diamonds in a hand with 16+ HCP. So rebid 2♠ with

♠ A Q J 7 ♥ 6 5 ♦ A K J 5 4 ♣ Q 4

5) Raising partner to 3♣

You	Partner
1♦	2♣
3♣	

♠ A 8 7 2 ♥ 5 ♦ A K 10 4 2 ♣ Q 4 3

A natural raise of clubs with at least three to an honor or four small in clubs. This is generally a minimum hand but can be very strong if nothing else fits:

♠ A K 7 ♥ 5 ♦ A K J 5 4 ♣ J 6 4 3

6) Rebidding 3NT

You	Partner
1♦	2♣
3NT	

♠ A J ♥ K J 6 ♦ A K J 10 6 5 4 ♣ 5

A 'source of tricks' rebid showing extra values (16+HCP) in a semi-balanced hand with 6+ near-to-solid diamonds plus stoppers in the unbid suits.

So then what happens?

Responder's continuations will generally be natural, keeping in mind that the auction is game-forcing. The partnership may have found a fit, or be ready to decide to play notrump. There still may be the possibility of finding a major-suit fit, and if so, that will still need exploration. At either player's third turn to call, if no suit has yet been agreed, new suits will usually be stopper-showing to test out the viability of notrump.

By the time we get this far into the auction, things can get pretty complex and the number of possible auctions is very large. Let's just look at a few examples:

Opener	Responder
♠ K Q 4	♠ A J 7
♥ 8 7	♥ 9 4
♦ A Q J 7 6 5	♦ K 4
♣ 9 4	♣ A Q J 8 7 6
1♦	2♣[1]
2♦[2]	3♣[3]
3♠[4]	4♦[5]
5♦[6]	

1. Natural and forcing to game
2. At least five diamonds
3. Extra club length
4. Spade stopper
5. Delayed diamond support, obviously no heart stopper
6. Looks like it has a chance – at least better than watching opponents reel off five (or more) heart tricks against 3NT

Opener	Responder
♠ 4 3	♠ A K 7 6
♥ A J 6 5	♥ 10 4
♦ A Q J 6 5	♦ 10 4
♣ 4 2	♣ A Q J 9 3
1♦	2♣[1]
2♦[2]	2♠[3]
2NT[4]	3NT[5]

1. Natural and game-forcing
2. At least five diamonds, likely nothing extra
3. Spades! Longer clubs
4. I have the unbid suit stopped
5. Looks like the right spot

Opener	Responder
♠ A Q 3	♠ K 8 7
♥ K J 7	♥ A 5 4
♦ K Q J 7 6	♦ 5
♣ Q 3	♣ A K J 10 5 4
1♦	2♣[1]
2NT[2]	3NT[3]
4NT[4]	6NT[5]

1. Natural, game-forcing
2. Usually balanced minimum 12-14 HCP but this time 18-19 HCP with stoppers in all unbid suits
3. Correct contract opposite the minimum
4. Quantitative. This time I've got the big one – what do you think?
5. Looks like a good bet for slam!

Summary

OPENER'S POSSIBLE REBIDS AFTER 1♦-2♣

2NT= 12-14 HCP, balanced or 18-19 HCP balanced, all unbid suits stopped

2♦ = 5+ diamonds, usually a minimum hand

3♦ = 6+ quality diamonds, 16+ HCP

3NT= 'source of tricks' — 6+ solid (or very nearly solid) diamonds — with stoppers in all unbid suits

3♣ = fit for clubs with at least three to an honor; may have extra values

2♥ or 2♠ = reverse, 16+ HCP, at least four cards in the major, longer diamonds

AFTER A ONE-LEVEL RESPONSE TO 1♣ OR 1♦

✓ Show a fit if one's been found (4-card support):
   Single raise = 12-15 HCP
   Double raise = 15-18 HCP
   Direct game raise = 18+ HCP, no shortness
   Splinter raise = 18+ HCP, show shortness by unusual jump

✓ Rebid notrump:
   1NT= 12-14 HCP
   2NT = 18-19 HCP
   3NT= source of tricks with stoppers

✓ Rebid own suit:
   Simple rebid = 5+ cards but almost always 6, minimum hand
   Jump rebid= 6+ cards, 16+ HCP, but invitational only

✓ Rebid new suit:
   Up the line = 12+ HCP
   Reverse=16+ HCP, forcing one round
   Jump Shift =18+ HCP, forcing to game

REBIDS AFTER MINOR-SUIT OPENINGS

NOW TRY THESE...

As you've probably surmised from the layout of the deals following, your assignment is to work out the correct bids for each player – just what you've always wanted to do – bid partner's cards for him!

1

Opener	Responder
♠ A Q 3 2	♠ K J 8 7
♥ K 7	♥ A 8 6 3
♦ 9 6 5	♦ 4 3
♣ A 9 5 3	♣ 10 8 2

2

Opener	Responder
♠ 9	♠ A 7 6 5
♥ A K J 6	♥ 9
♦ Q J 5 4	♦ K 10
♣ K 8 7 6	♣ A Q J 10 5 2

3

Opener	Responder
♠ K 8	♠ Q 5 4 3
♥ K Q J 9	♥ A 10 5 4
♦ A 5	♦ 9 6 2
♣ A Q 8 7 2	♣ 9 4

4

Opener	Responder
♠ 7	♠ 9 5 4
♥ A J 8 7	♥ K Q 10 5
♦ A K 8 7 6 2	♦ 9
♣ 8 2	♣ A K Q 7 6

5

Opener	Responder
♠ Q 7 6	♠ J 9 5 4
♥ A Q 3	♥ 9 2
♦ Q J 10 5 4	♦ K 7
♣ K 8	♣ A Q J 5 4

6

Opener	Responder
♠ A K 10 5 4	♠ 9 8 2
♥ 7	♥ A Q 9 4
♦ A K Q 4 3 2	♦ J 9 6 5
♣ 5	♣ J 6

7

Opener	Responder
♠ K 8 7	♠ A Q J
♥ J 7	♥ K Q 9 3
♦ A 6 5	♦ K Q J
♣ A 10 8 7 2	♣ J 9 3

8

Opener	Responder
♠ A 3	♠ Q 10 5 4
♥ A J 7	♥ Q 6
♦ A K J 10 5 4	♦ 9 2
♣ 8 7	♣ Q 10 9 5 4

9

Opener	Responder
♠ J 8 7	♠ 10 5 4
♥ A Q 4 3	♥ K 9
♦ A Q 3 2	♦ K 9
♣ 8 7	♣ A K J 10 6 5

10

Opener	Responder
♠ A Q 10 6 5	♠ J 7 2
♥ A	♥ Q 9 8 7 3
♦ 6	♦ K J 7
♣ A K J 10 7 2	♣ 4 3

ANSWERS

1

Opener	Responder
1♣	1♥[1]
1♠[2]	2♠[3]
pass[4]	

1. Up the line response.
2. Continuing the search for a fit.
3. I have 4 spades and a weak invitation.
4. Minimum for me, too.

2

Opener	Responder
1♦[1]	2♣[2]
3♠[3]	4NT[4]
5♦	6♣
pass	

1. With 4-4 in the minors and potential rebid problems (after 1♣-1♠) the diamond opening is more flexible.
2. Game-forcing Two-over-One.
3. Splinter raise of clubs.
4. Looks like good fit, Aces?

3

Opener	Responder
1♣[1]	1♥[2]
4♥[3]	pass

1. Normal opening albeit with extras.
2. Up-the-line, 4+ cards, 6+HCP
3. Direct game raise with 18+ HCP, 4-card support and no side suit shortness.

4

Opener	Responder
1♦	2♣[1]
2♦[2]	2♥[3]
3♥[4]	4♣[5]
4NT[6]	5♦
6♥	pass

1. Game-forcing Two-over-One response.
2. Not enough strength for reverse to 2♥.
3. Hearts as well as clubs.
4. I also have hearts.
5. Cuebid – club control.
6. Aces?

5

Opener	Responder
1♦	1♠[1]
1NT[2]	2NT[3]
3NT[4]	pass

1. Up the line, not enough HCP for a game-forcing 2♣.
2. 12-14 HCP, balanced.
3. Invitational raise.
4. I have a maximum.

6

Opener	Responder
1♦[1]	1♥[2]
1♠[3]	2♦[4]
2♠[5]	3♠[6]
4♠[7]	pass

1. Longer suit first.
2. Up the line.
3. I also have 4+ spades.
4. I prefer diamonds and don't have any extra strength, heart length or club stopper to show.
5. Surprise, I have a fifth spade and therefore a sixth diamond.
6. I have 3-card support for your second suit.
7. I have enough for game.

7

Opener	Responder
1♣	1♥[1]
1NT[2]	4NT[3]
pass[4]	

1. Up the line.
2. 12-14 HCP, balanced, without four spades or four hearts.
3. Quantitative raise, inviting slam.
4. Sorry, I'm minimum (as usual!).

8

Opener	Responder
1♦	1♠
3♦[1]	pass[2]

1. Extra values (16+HCP), extra diamonds, but only invitational.
2. Nothing extra over here!

9

Opener	Responder
1♦	2♣[1]
2NT[2]	3NT[3]
pass[4]	

1. Game-forcing.
2. Balanced minimum, would like to have both majors stopped but que sera…
3. Looks like the best spot.
4. Sure, my club finesses always work.

10

Opener	Responder
1♣[1]	1♥
2♠[2]	2NT[3]
3♠[4]	4♠[5]
pass	

1. Longer suit first.
2. Jump shift, natural and game-forcing but only promising four spades for the time being.
3. No real fit yet but I do have a diamond stopper.
4. I have a fifth spade and therefore a sixth club.
5. I have 3-card support but nothing extra.

AFTER NOTRUMP RESPONSES TO MINORS

♥ There is one thing I insist upon, and that is for partners to tell each other their strength. *Criticus.* **Contract Simplicitas.** *1933.*

At least in theory, the auctions in this section should be among the least complex you can conduct after a minor-suit opening bid. The range of values and distributions for notrump responses are very narrowly defined and that does in fact simplify matters a great deal. Once again, there's no need for any real variance from what you've been playing as part of your Standard system, so this chapter is going to be mostly a summary of what you already know. There are a couple of points I want to make, though…

Normally in these auctions you're going to end up playing in notrump, or, less frequently, in one of opener's suits if he is unbalanced. One of the main things you need to check on, therefore, is whether you have stoppers in unbid suits, especially the majors. There's not a lot of fun to be had by having the values for game but landing in three notrump and watching the defenders reel off five or six tricks in an unstopped suit. As much as is practical, we'll try to avoid that happening to you.

After a 1NT response

You | **Partner**
1♣ *or* 1♦ | 1NT
? |

Since this response shows relative weakness (6-9 HCP) and no 4-card major plus no 5-card support for your minor, the way to proceed will often be very clear. Remember, unlike the 1NT response to a major-suit opening, this 1NT bid is not forcing at all.

With a minimum hand, you have three options:

- With all balanced or semi-balanced hands without values for the possibility of game, pass. Don't fear unstopped suits – it's only a 7-trick contract!

- With a 6-card or longer minor suit and minimum values, rebid your suit.

- If you have opened 1♦ with length in both minors, you can make a simple club rebid to get partner to choose which minor he prefers, usually for a partscore. This rebid is not forcing so be careful not to make it if your hand has serious game potential opposite a maximum 1NT response.

With a medium-strength hand (15-17 HCP):

- You can raise to 2NT as an invitational call, usually with a hand that you didn't like for an original 1NT opening.

- You can jump rebid your own suit as an invitational call. This will usually show a 6+ card suit of decent quality and about 15-17 HCP. Partner is encouraged, although not forced, to continue towards a possible 3NT contract, particularly with an honor in your suit and a maximum 1NT. Partner can continue by bidding a new suit as a stopper-showing acceptance of the invitation.

- You can make a reverse into a new suit — usually a major but 1♣-1NT-2♦ also qualifies. With stoppers in the unbid suits and a maximum, partner can go straight to 3NT. If, as is more often the case, he has only one of the unbid suits stopped, he can show which one by bidding it. Remember, partner has already denied 4+card length in a major by his initial response so bidding a major at his second turn will not be an attempt to find a fit in that suit.

With a strong hand (18+ HCP):

- The simplest auction will occur when you have a balanced 18-19 HCP hand and you simply raise to 3NT.

- You could have a game-going hand and still make a reverse rebid as a probe to make sure there are stoppers in all suits.

- There is only one jump shift auction that can occur in this context and that is 1♦-1NT-3♣. This rebid is natural and game forcing and gives partner some choices in his followup. Frequently he will simply take a preference to diamonds and see what you have to say next. He can also rebid notrump with both majors stopped and no great potential for a high-level minor-suit contract or he can rebid three of a major, ostensibly to show that suit stopped and the other major unstopped.

After a 2NT response

Again there will be few surprises here:

> **You**   **Partner**
> 1♣ *or* 1♦   2NT
> ?

- With a minimum balanced hand in the 12-13 HCP range, you should simply pass and reject the invitation.

- With a balanced or semi-balanced hand with 13+ HCP, you raise to 3NT.

- A rebid of your minor at the 3-level is generally best played as a sign-off — 'I think three of my minor is a better contract than 2NT' — thus showing an unbalanced hand with 6+ cards in the minor.

- A reverse into a new suit is an acceptance of the game invitation usually showing a stopper and an unbalanced hand, trying to make sure the right game is reached. Partner's below-game continuations will also focus on stoppers.

> **BY THE WAY**
>
> *Some bidding theorists maintain that any rebid by opener over the invitational 2NT response should create a force on both partners. You can decide which approach suits your partnership best but, on balance, the retreat to a more sensible partscore seems advisable to me.*

After a 3NT response

> **You**   **Partner**
> 1♣ *or* 1♦   3NT
> ?

Largely because so much space has already been used up, your most frequent action will be to pass. Remember, partner has promised stoppers in all unbid suits to go with his 15-17 HCP so you need not be (overly) concerned about unstopped suits.

- Any advance you make past 3NT will be a try for slam.

- A simple rebid of the minor shows extra length (6+cards) and invites a cuebid. Partner with a dearth of controls and low slam potential may sign off in 4NT (which is not Blackwood!).

- A new suit bid shows an unbalanced hand. Again, partner's forward move would be a cuebid, with a return to 4NT showing lack of interest.

- A raise to 4NT is quantitative with about 16-17 HCP and presumably a hand that was flawed for an original 1NT opening.

Summary

✓ After auctions that start with a 1♣ or 1♦ opening and a notrump response the partnership will usually play in notrump, somewhat less frequently in opener's minor and even less frequently in a new suit introduced by opener. Any chance responder might have had to introduce a suit as a potential trump suit is gone!

✓ Stopper showing and seeking will usually be a prime concern of the follow-up auction.

✓ Opener's non-jump rebid of his opened minor after a 1NT or 2NT response is a sign-off – Stop, partner! After 3NT, a rebid of the minor is a try for slam.

AFTER NOTRUMP RESPONSES TO MINORS

NOW TRY THESE...

With each of the following hands you've opened 1♣. What is your rebid after each of the following responses (a) 1NT? (b) 2NT? (c) 3NT?

1   ♠ A 4 3   ♥ 5   ♦ K J 8   ♣ A J 10 6 5 4

2   ♠ A Q 3 2   ♥ K J 7 6   ♦ 6 2   ♣ A 7 6

3   ♠ 4   ♥ K 4 3   ♦ A J 6   ♣ A K J 10 5 4

4   ♠ A Q 7 6   ♥ 6   ♦ 5 4   ♣ A K 7 6 5 2

For each of the following pairs of hands, try to create the complete auction:

5

Opener	Responder
♠ 4	♠ J 7 6
♥ K Q 3	♥ A 4 2
♦ A 4 3	♦ Q J 6
♣ A K J 10 5 4	♣ 9 7 3 2

6

Opener	Responder
♠ A 4 3	♠ K J 8
♥ 8	♥ Q J 7
♦ A Q 8 7 4	♦ 9 6 3
♣ K J 7 6	♣ A 10 5 4

7

Opener	Responder
♠ K Q 4 3	♠ A 8 7
♥ A Q J 8	♥ K 9 4
♦ 7	♦ J 9 2
♣ A Q 7 6	♣ J 9 3 2

8

Opener	Responder
♠ A 3	♠ K 9 4
♥ 7	♥ Q 10 9
♦ K Q J	♦ A 7 6 5
♣ A Q J 7 6 5 4	♣ K 8 2

ANSWERS

1 a) 2♣ Looks like a better partscore from over here.

b) 3NT Enough values to accept the invitation but maybe not quite enough overall strength for an eleven-trick contract that the scientists among you might get to 5♣ by rebidding 2♦ and finding out partner doesn't have a heart stopper. I concur with whichever choice works this time! In other words, no approach is perfect all the time!

c) 4♣ This time it's clear to move forward and issue a slam invitation via 4♣. You're hoping to hear partner cuebid 4♦ over which you'll continue with a 4♠ cuebid, but if he disappoints you by rebidding 4NT respect his signoff and pass.

2 a) Pass Balanced minimum, nowhere to go.

b) 3NT With 14 HCP you have enough for game and really have no safe way to explore for a diamond stopper as there is no obvious alternative strain to play in if you don't find one. Who leads a minor suit when there are two unbid majors anyway?

c) Pass Obvious to you, I hope!

3 a) 3♣ A natural invitational rebid. With a maximum, partner may be able to make another move.

b) 3♦ Put partner in stopper-showing mode. If he rebids 3♠ (spade stopper, no heart stopper) or 3NT (both majors stopped), 3NT will look right. However, if he rebids 3♥ (heart stopper, no spade stopper), a small slam in clubs looks very likely.

c) 4♣ Set the suit, and see what partner does. Depending on partner's number of aces and kings, you should be able to count winners for either the small or grand slam.

4 a) 2♣ You should give up on spades as the best fit you can hope for in that suit is a 4-3.

b) 3♠ This time you do want to bid your hand naturally as you have enough values to go to game but it's not yet clear what the strain should be.

c) 4♣ Your shape and controls make you worth one try. If partner bids 4NT, you will respect his decision and pass.

	Opener	**Responder**	
5	1♣	1NT	1. Natural, invitational.
	3♣[1]	3♦[2]	2. Diamond stopper.
	3♥[3]	4♣[4]	3. Heart stopper.
	5♣[5]	pass[6]	4. No spade stopper, some club support.

5. Looks like enough.
6. Okay, just glad I wasn't in 3NT losing the first five or six spade tricks!

	Opener	**Responder**	
6	1♦	2NT[1]	1. 11-12 HCP, invitational to game.
	3NT[2]	pass[3]	

2. Enough to accept but not enough overall strength to probe for stoppers as an alternative contract of five of a minor looks too high. Hope you can look after hearts.
3. Not to worry, I always guess these two-way club finesses right, especially after a spade lead!

	Opener	**Responder**	
7	1♣	1NT	1. Hearts stopped, what about you?
	2♥[1]	2♠[2]	2. Spades stopped, no diamond stopper else I would have rebid notrump.
	3♠[3]	5♣[4]	
	pass		

3. I have spades as well – are you getting a good picture of my distribution?
4. Looks like the right game.

	Opener	**Responder**	
8	1♣	2NT[1]	1. 11-12 HCP, game invitation.
	3♦[2]	3NT[3]	2. Diamond values, what have you got?
	4♣[4]	4♦[5]	3. Both majors stopped.
	4♠[6]	6♣[7]	4. I really rebid 3♦ to set up this call, a slam try with really good and long clubs.
	pass		

5. Okay, I have a good club fit and the diamond ace.
6. Spade cuebid.
7. With a spade card, the diamond ace and a trump honor, I must have everything you need for slam.

AFTER A MINOR
SUIT IS RAISED

♥ Hope is a good assistant when hope is promising, and a bad one when hope is faint. *Criticus.* **Contract Simplicitas.** *1933.*

In general, after your minor-suit opening bid has attracted a raise, the rebids are somewhat similar to those after an initial notrump response. The focus is once again on getting to three notrump as the most probable game — mainly because of the old saw that 'nine tricks are easier than eleven', but also with a certain homage being paid to the scoring table.

The most significant difference is that, although the suit is one of the lowly minors, a fit has been found and this impacts the subsequent bidding in two ways. First, there's a refuge to return to — if the stopper seeking/showing exercise reveals a serious chink in your joint armor, you can always play in the minor suit. Second, you can often proceed in the expectation that the agreed minor suit will produce five tricks due to partner's promised length. For example, if you open 1♣ holding ♣AKQ3, and partner raises, you know his HCP are elsewhere; but you also know partner will be a favorite to hold five cards in the suit to justify raising, so five club tricks are there for the taking in notrump.

Virtually without exception, all simple new suit bids below game by either partner are stopper-showing for notrump purposes: 'I have this suit stopped, what do you have?' Except with very rare distributional hands, you will never want to play in an alternative suit.

After a single raise

You	Partner	You	Partner
1♣	2♣	1♦	2♦

Since partner is limited to 6-9 HCP and will generally have at least some of his scant values in the raised suit, you shouldn't expect to find more than one outside stopper in partner's hand and should proceed on that basis.

With all hands in the minimum opening range you should pass! You've found a fit, game is unlikely, so quit while you're ahead. Don't fall victim to 'But I have only have three clubs' short-minor paranoia or 'But notrump scores more' duplicate-itis.

Very strong hands, whether balanced, unbalanced or in-between, that have a reasonable expectation of taking nine tricks, without losing five first, should proceed directly to 3NT as the likeliest game.

With close to game-going values in a balanced or semi-balanced hand with stoppers in the outside suits, you can make the general strength game try of 2NT. This asks partner to carry on with anything more than a bare minimum single raise but lets him off the hook if he's cheated a little and raised to obstruct the opponents a little without full values. He can signify this dog of a hand by returning to three of your minor.

With near game values but a glaring hole stopper-wise, you can bid a new suit (forcing) to show a stopper in the suit bid and simultaneously ask for partner's co-operation. Rarely should you expect to find partner with more than one outside stopper.

After a limit raise

You	Partner	You	Partner
1♣	3♣	1♦	3♦
?		?	

Again, your new suit rebids will be stopper-showing and asking partner to cooperate by showing his stopper(s) up the line. Due to partner's known strength (10-12 HCP), you will occasionally find him with more than one outside stopper. In any event, you will need to have more than a minimum opening bid to try for game since the limit raise will generally mean the partnership has already reached their combined trick-taking limit at three of the minor unless you have extra values (14+ HCP).

So after 1♣-3♣, pass with

♠ A Q 4 3   ♥ K 9 4   ♦ K 8 4   ♣ J 8 7

and also pass with

♠ A K Q 4   ♥ 7 6 5   ♦ Q 3   ♣ Q 8 7 3

— it's too much to expect partner to have stoppers for both red suits and enough in clubs for that suit to also run. But with

♠ 6 5 4   ♥ A Q J   ♦ K 10 4   ♣ A 8 7 2

rebid 3♦ to show that stopper, hoping to hear that partner has spades stopped. It's not just a matter of
strength; with

♠ Q J 7 ♥ A J 7 ♦ A 7 3 ♣ Q 10 5 4

you should rebid 3NT (all suits stopped – go for it!)
while with

♠ A K 8 ♥ 6 5 3 ♦ A 4 ♣ A K J 8 7

(a much better hand) you should rebid 3♦ to show
your stopper and hope to hear 3♥ from partner.

With a really big hand, you will continue on past
3NT or four of the minor. By so doing, you modify the
meaning of your first rebid to mean 'I was really interested in slam all along – what say you now?'

After a Criss-Cross forcing raise

You	Partner	You	Partner
1♣	2♦	1♦	3♣
?		?	

BY THE WAY

*As you can see from the
examples, opener can have a wide
range for his ostensible game
tries. You need to be able to play
in four of the agreed minor if the
right stoppers aren't located and
opener isn't strong enough to
underwrite eleven tricks in a
minor. The key principle to keep in
mind in all of this is that opener
will be the captain who decides
what level to play at since the
responder's limits are more
narrowly defined.*

This time partner has forced to game and the only questions to be resolved
are (a) which game – the minor or notrump? And (b) is slam possible?

Since our priority is always 'game first' and 'notrump before a minor', you
should rebid notrump whenever you have scattered values in a balanced hand
with at least most of the unbid suits stopped. Most particularly you need the
unbid majors stopped (that seems to be what the $%**&* opponents lead when
you don't have them stopped!).

So, after 1♣-2♦ with

♠ A Q 3 ♥ J 10 5 4 ♦ K 8 ♣ K 6 5 4

rebid 2NT, while with

♠ K 7 ♥ A Q 4 3 ♦ J 8 7 6 ♣ K 7 6

rebid 3NT after 1♦-3♣.

New suit bids are stopper-showing and partner is asked to cooperate in the
notrump quest by showing his outside stopper(s). With both unbid suits
stopped, partner can logically bid notrump right away while with one stopped
and not the other, he can show the one he does have stopped if it is convenient
to do so below game.

A useful temporizing stratagem is to rebid your minor with a very good
hand, and wait to see what partner does. Remember, he can't pass!

You	Partner
1♦	3♣
?	

♠ A K 7 ♥ Q 3 2 ♦ A K J 10 8 5 ♣ 7

3♦ would be a good first move; you'll get really excited if partner can bid 3♥!

Summary

✓ After a direct raise of a minor-suit opening, the order of priority is 'game first' and 'notrump before the minor'.

✓ New suit bids below game by both players are stopper-showing tries for notrump – at least until proven otherwise!

✓ By bidding a new suit beyond three notrump, either partner will normally be making a slam try and showing a control in the bid suit.

✓ After a Criss-Cross forcing raise, the rebid of the agreed suit is a useful temporizing move that allows efficient use of auction space.

AFTER A MINOR SUIT IS RAISED

NOW TRY THESE...

What is your next bid in each case?

1
- ♠ A Q 4 3
- ♥ 7 5
- ♦ A J 7
- ♣ K 10 5 4

You	Partner
1♣	2♣
?	

2
- ♠ A Q 4 3
- ♥ 7 5
- ♦ A J 7
- ♣ K 10 5 4

You	Partner
1♣	3♣
?	

3
- ♠ A Q 4 3
- ♥ 7 5
- ♦ A J 7
- ♣ K 10 5 4

You	Partner
1♣	2♦
?	

4
- ♠ A 4
- ♥ K 8
- ♦ A Q 7 6 5
- ♣ 9 7 5 4

You	Partner
1♦	2♦
?	

5
- ♠ A 4
- ♥ K 8
- ♦ A Q 7 6 5
- ♣ 9 7 5 4

You	Partner
1♦	3♦
?	

6
- ♠ A 4
- ♥ K 8
- ♦ A Q 7 6 5
- ♣ 9 7 5 4

You	Partner
1♦	3♣
?	

Construct a recommended auction for the following pairs of hands:

7

Opener	Responder
♠ A Q 6 5	♠ 8 7
♥ 9 7 5 2	♥ 6 4 3
♦ A J 7	♦ K Q 9 5 4
♣ K 8	♣ A Q 4

8

Opener	Responder
♠ A	♠ K J 7
♥ J 8 7 6	♥ 9 4
♦ K Q 4	♦ A J 8
♣ A Q 8 7 6	♣ K J 10 3 2

9

Opener	Responder
♠ A Q 3	♠ K 4
♥ 9	♥ 8 6 5
♦ A J 8 7 4	♦ K 10 9 6 2
♣ A K 10 3	♣ 9 7 5

10

Opener	Responder
♠ 8 7	♠ 9 5 2
♥ A Q 9 4	♥ K 6
♦ A 9	♦ K J 8
♣ A J 8 7 6	♣ K Q 9 4 3

ANSWERS

1 Pass A balanced minimum.

2 3♦ Try for 3NT by showing your diamond stopper hoping partner can show a heart stopper. Remember he has a maximum of three hearts so it would be a bad gamble to shoot out 3NT if there was no semblance of a stopper between you. If he rebids 3♠ to show a stopper there, 5♣ looks like a good chance while if he returns to 4♣ that will mean nothing in either major so that his side-suit values, although scant, will be in diamonds (say ♠87 ♥964 ♦KQ6 ♣AQ972) which will also make 5♣ a reasonable gamble.

3 2♠ To show your stoppers in a way that is the most economical use of the auction space, i.e. the 'cheapest bid', not necessarily the lowest-ranked suit.

4 Pass A good hand but not enough combined material to make any game sensible.

5 3NT With both majors stopped and some protective club length, this seems like a reasonable shot at game.

6 3♦ Leave partner room to bid 3♥ if possible and then you can continue with 3♠ leaving the next decision up to him.

7

Opener	Responder
1♦	3♦[1]
3NT[2]	pass

1. Limit raise.
2. Stoppers plus some heart length as protection.

8

Opener	Responder
1♣	2♦[1]
3♦[2]	3♠[3]
3NT[4]	pass

1. Game-forcing club raise.
2. Diamond stopper.
3. Spade stopper.
4. That's what I wanted to hear

9

Opener	Responder
1♦	2♦[1]
2♠[2]	3♦[3]
4♣[4]	4♠[5]
6♦[6]	pass

1. 6-9 HCP, 5 diamonds.
2. Game try, spades stopped.
3. Nothing in clubs or hearts.
4. Still trying, but now for 5♦.
5. I do have a side card — in spades.
6 The truly conservative might bid only 5♦ but the fit looks excellent!

10

Opener	Responder
1♣	3♣[1]
3♦[2]	3♥[3]
5♣[4]	pass

1. Limit raise.
2. Diamonds stopped.
3. Hearts stopped, but not spades (would have bid 3NT).
4. Er… we seem to be missing a spade control, but game should still be on.

FOURTH SUIT FORCING (FSF)

♥ If an individual player elects to use this convention with a partner who is familiar with it, he will find it a very fascinating bid with great possibilities. **The Official System of Contract Bridge.** *1931.*

Each of the next four Steps will be considered 'Advanced' or perhaps 'too fancy' by some readers and, to a certain extent, those labels are justified. The ideas in them are by no means mandatory, but if you add them to your system (whether or not you decide to adopt the Two-over-One approach), you'll find them useful and enjoyable gadgets. Stick with me just a little bit longer and I'm sure you'll find what is described in these Steps is philosophically and practically consistent with our stated goals:

- *To find and exploit major suit fits to the fullest*
- *To emphasize notrump over minor-suit games*
- *Whenever possible to conduct at least part of our slam exploration below the game level*
- *To avoid being in notrump games with unstopped suits.*

I think those of you with a more enlightened or scientific outlook will soon agree that the contents of these four Steps are not only fun and useful but virtually indispensable in the furtherance of our bidding goals.

FOURTH-SUIT
FORCING (FSF)

OK, I'll go along for now. What's the first gadget?

The first one comes up when responder is an unpassed hand and the first three calls in the auction are all in different suits, with no-one having jumped, as in these examples:

Partner	You		Partner	You
1♣	1♥		1♦	1♠
1♠	?		2♣	?

These aren't Two-over-One auctions, and we often don't know much yet about the strain we want to play in or what level we want to get to. Continuations you might be considering include:

- *Inviting or forcing to game in your suit, one of partner's suits or notrump.*

- *Looking for 3-card support for your own major suit.*

- *Looking for a stopper in the unbid suit.*

- *Sending a below-game slam-possibility signal.*

- *Signing off in a partscore in your suit or one of partner's suits.*

While it's true that the bidding language we have to work with is an imperfect tool, reaching all of those goals and many more can be enhanced by adopting Fourth Suit Forcing (FSF).

BY THE WAY

Some writers advocate making exceptions to the 100% forcing to game rule but I have found that this only diminishes the clarity and effectiveness of FSF auctions. Stick to the game-forcing approach and email me at Thurston@computan.on.ca with any apparently insoluble problems this causes you.

Here's the definition of this convention:

> **When 3 suits have been bid and an unpassed hand responder makes a simple bid of the fourth suit, that call is artificial (it doesn't promise any length or strength in the fourth suit) and 100% forcing to game.**

Your second bid is FSF in each of these auctions:

Partner	You		Partner	You
1♣	1♥		1♥	1♠
1♠	2♦		2♦	3♣

While I try not to burden you with exceptions, this is one instance where an exception can't be avoided. This sequence:

Partner	You
1♣	1♦
1♥	1♠

is not FSF but rather a natural up-the-line continuation that shows at least four spades and is forcing for one round only. You can use FSF in this sequence by jumping instead to 2♠ at your second turn.

Cute — but what does it mean?

You will always have game-forcing values (at least an opening bid) and will generally have at least one of the following reasons to use FSF:

1. You have a 5-card major (sometimes 6+) and you are seeking 3-card support (sometimes a doubleton honor). For example:

    ♠ J 6 ♥ K Q 10 7 5 ♦ A J 7 ♣ K 9 8

Partner	You
1♣	1♥
1♠	2♦

2. You have values sufficient for game but no stopper in the fourth suit for notrump purposes:

    ♠ K 8 7 ♥ A Q 3 2 ♦ 7 4 3 ♣ K J 7

Partner	You
1♣	1♥
1♠	2♦

3. You have support for one of partner's suits and wish to show it at the same time as you advise partner that slam may be a possibility. For example:

    ♠ K 8 ♥ A Q 3 2 ♦ A 3 ♣ K J 7 6 3

Partner	You
1♣	1♥
1♠	2♦

    Having created the game-force by bidding 2♦, you can support clubs next round without fear of having partner pass.

In addition to those three prime motivations for using FSF, there are many offshoot benefits in the form of meanings that apply when you don't use FSF! In particular, all second-round jumps, either in notrump or a previously bid suit, are invitational only. Examples of this are:

♠ 7 6 ♥ A Q 4 3 ♦ K Q 6 5 4 ♣ 10 2

Partner	You
1♦	1♥
1♠	3♦

A diamond limit raise that had hearts to show.

♠ 4 3 ♥ A Q 3 2 ♦ J 8 7 ♣ K J 10 2

Partner	You
1♦	1♥
1♠	2NT

10-12 HCP with four (maybe five) hearts and clubs (the unbid suit) stopped.

♠ Q 2 ♥ A Q 10 5 4 3 ♦ 6 5 ♣ K 7 6

Partner	You
1♦	1♥
1♠	3♥

An invitational strength hand with 6+ hearts and about 10-12 HCP.

♠ K J 3 2 ♥ A K 3 2 ♦ 4 3 ♣ 10 4 3

Partner	You
1♦	1♥
1♠	3♠

This would show a fairly serious game invitation in spades with 4-card support and about 9-12 HCP.

And then what happens?

After responder makes the FSF bid, opener's choices for his third call will go a long way towards resolving the issue of strain and somewhat help in the matter of game or slam.

In order of priority, opener should:

1) Show 3-card support for responder's first-bid major.

2) Show a stopper in the fourth suit by bidding notrump.

3) Rebid a 5+card suit of his own if it's at least good quality.

4) When none of the above are possible, opener may have to 'raise' the fourth suit. While this is admittedly rare, it can solve the dilemma of what to do with

♠ A Q 3 2 ♥ 7 6 ♦ 6 5 4 ♣ A K 7 6

when the auction starts

You	Partner
1♣	1♥
1♠	2♦
?	

If you rebid 3♦ at least it conveys all the things you don't have: a third heart, a fifth club or a diamond stopper – perfect!

Summary

While some confusion will be inevitable in your initial gropings with FSF, just keep these guidelines in mind:

✓ FSF is a warm, happy bid that says 'We're going to game, at least, partner, now let's try to figure out which game and whether we're on for slam.'

✓ You want to find an eight-card major suit fit if it's there to be found.

✓ You don't want to be in 3NT with an unstopped suit, especially the 'unbid' suit if you can help it because that's the lead they always make!

✓ Bidding space is precious and any below-game slam exploration you can accomplish is a good use of that space.

FOURTH SUIT FORCING (FSF)

NOW TRY THESE...

Let's do some more 'construct the auction' exercises and in the process we'll get you a little more comfortable with FSF (and when FSF might have been, but wasn't, used!). Note: all the hands in this section come from actual competitions – they are not 'cooked' to fit the system. In some cases, I wish they had been!

1 *Opener*   *Responder*
- ♠ K 7 6 4   ♠ Q J 7
- ♥ A J 6   ♥ K 10 9 4
- ♦ 9 2   ♦ A 10 4
- ♣ A Q 5 4   ♣ K 9 7

2 *Opener*   *Responder*
- ♠ A 9 7 6   ♠ 8
- ♥ 8   ♥ A Q 3 2
- ♦ A 10 4   ♦ K 8 7
- ♣ K Q 9 7 5   ♣ A J 8 4 2

3 *Opener*   *Responder*
- ♠ A Q 9 6   ♠ J 8 7
- ♥ K 9   ♥ A Q 8 7 5 3
- ♦ 9 5 2   ♦ A 4
- ♣ A J 8 7   ♣ K 4

4 *Opener*   *Responder*
- ♠ A Q 9 6   ♠ K J 8 4
- ♥ 8 7   ♥ A K 10 5 4
- ♦ K 7 6   ♦ A 3
- ♣ Q J 7 6   ♣ 9 4

5 *Opener*   *Responder*
- ♠ K 8 7 4   ♠ A 6
- ♥ 9 3   ♥ A K Q 10 4
- ♦ A Q 6   ♦ K J 7
- ♣ K Q 4 3   ♣ J 9 7

6 *Opener*   *Responder*
- ♠ K J 8 7   ♠ Q 4
- ♥ Q 5 4   ♥ A J 10 3
- ♦ 7 4   ♦ K J 9
- ♣ A Q 4 3   ♣ 10 8 7 2

7 *Opener*   *Responder*
- ♠ 8 5   ♠ A Q 9 4
- ♥ 10 4   ♥ 9 5
- ♦ A Q 9 6 5   ♦ K J 8 3 2
- ♣ A Q 3 2   ♣ J 7

8 *Opener*   *Responder*
- ♠ Q 2   ♠ A J 10 5 4 3
- ♥ 6   ♥ Q 9 4
- ♦ A Q 6 5 4   ♦ K 8
- ♣ A J 7 5 4   ♣ 9 2

9 *Opener*   *Responder*
- ♠ 7   ♠ A Q 8 6 2
- ♥ 10 5 4 3   ♥ K 9
- ♦ A K 8 7   ♦ J 5 4
- ♣ A Q 9 2   ♣ K 8 3

10 *Opener*   *Responder*
- ♠ K 8   ♠ 9 5 2
- ♥ K 6 5 2   ♥ A J
- ♦ Q 4   ♦ A K 7 6 5
- ♣ A J 9 5 4   ♣ Q 6 2

11 *Opener*   *Responder*
- ♠ K 8 7   ♠ A Q 10 5 4
- ♥ 6   ♥ A J 5
- ♦ A Q 8 6 3   ♦ 10 4
- ♣ A Q 3 2   ♣ 9 7 5

ANSWERS

1

Opener	Responder
1♣	1♥
1♠	2♦[1]
2♥[2]	2NT[3]
3NT[4]	pass[5]

1. FSF.
2. 3-card support.
3. Heart support wasn't really what I was looking for. Anything else you can tell me?
4. Sorry, just the typical balanced junkbox, glad you've got diamonds stopped.
5. Looks like our best bet for game.

2

Opener	Responder
1♣	1♥
1♠	2♦[1]
2NT[2]	3♣[3]
3♦[4]	3♥[5]
3♠[5]	4♦[5]
4♥[5]	4♠[5]
6♣[6]	pass

1. FSF.
2. Diamonds stopped.
3. Forcing raise in clubs (with at least four hearts). What do you think about a club slam?
4. I like the idea and I have a diamond control.
5. Cuebid.
6. I'm worn out and this looks like enough, I've bid my all.

3

Opener	Responder
1♣	1♥
1♠	2♦[1]
3♦[2]	3♥[3]
4♥[4]	pass[5]

1. FSF.
2. No 3-card heart support, no diamond stopper, no fifth club, Help!
3. I have six hearts, how does that suit you?
4. Great, I have a doubleton honor.
5. Must be the right game.

4

Opener	Responder
1♣	1♥
1♠	2♦[1]
2NT[2]	3♠[3]
4♠[4]	pass[5]

1. FSF.
2. I have a diamond stopper.
3. But I have a game-forcing spade raise with just enough to ask you about slam.
4. Thanks for the raise but I have a dead minimum.
5. At least I found all this out below game!

5

Opener	Responder
1♣	1♥
1♠	2♦[1]
2NT[2]	4NT[3]
6NT[4]	pass

1. FSF.
2. Diamonds stopped.
3. I know you're likely in the 12-14 HCP range so, assuming that, this is a quantitative raise of notrump – are you closer to 12 or 14?
4. Tip-top 14 HCP.

6

Opener	Responder
1♣	1♥
1♠	2NT[1]
pass[2]	

1. Invitational in notrump.
2. Sorry, minimum as usual. Note that opener doesn't show his 3-card heart support, something he might do on the way to game if he had enough (14 HCP+) to accept the invitation.

7	Opener	Responder	1. Delayed limit raise with 5+ diamonds, 4+ spades and invitational values.
	1♦	1♠	2. Invitation cheerfully declined!
	2♣	3♦[1]	
	pass[2]		

8	Opener	Responder	1. Invitational with the focus on spades.
	1♦	1♠	2. Enough to accept with a doubleton trump, aces and a ruffing value. Note that if opener's majors were reversed his proper move would be to pass, not bid more clubs, since responder doesn't seem interested in anything but spades.
	2♣	3♠[1]	
	4♠[2]	pass	

9	Opener	Responder	1. FSF.
	1♦	1♠	2. Raising the fourth suit is the natural thing to do, especially with length and no stopper.
	2♣	2♥[1]	3. Spades look to be out of the picture and I do have something in hearts with the lead coming up to my hand.
	3♥[2]	3NT[3]	
	pass[4]		4. Looks ugly but nothing else looks better.

10	Opener	Responder	1. FSF.
	1♣	1♦	2. Spades stopped.
	1♥	2♠[1]	3. Another somewhat ugly game but at least as good as anything else.
	2NT[2]	3NT[3]	4. From the right side anyway!
	pass[4]		

11	Opener	Responder	1. Natural game try.
	1♦	1♠	2. Enough to accept the try and oh, by the way, I have 3-card spade support.
	2♣	2NT[1]	3. Looks better than notrump (maybe).
	3♠[2]	4♠[3]	
	pass		

Note: Hand 11 is the type of set-up that those who want to play FSF as not always 100% forcing to game point to — the 5-3 spade fit might get lost. As long as opener has enough to accept any invitational sequence, he can always 'check back' by showing his spade support along the way to game.

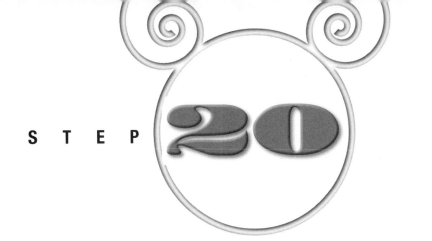

STEP **20**

WEAK JUMP SHIFTS

If the Steps you're learning were part of a dance class, the music to accompany this section would be decidedly up-tempo. As you'll soon see, 'Weak Jump Shifts' (WJS) are both fun and practical, but they're definitely not for the faint-hearted.

Playing Two-over-One, we need no longer wait for the somewhat rare and auction-space consuming classic requirements of a hand with a good suit and game-forcing, slam-invitational values to use the jump shift. So far, you've seen innovative uses for minor-suit jump shifts over major-suit openings (Bergen raises) and over minor-suit openings (Criss-Cross forcing minor raises). Also along the way, we found a new use for the sequence 1♠-3♥ — natural and invitational.

The only initial jump shift responses we haven't mentioned yet are major-suit jump shifts after minor-suit openings and spades over hearts in the start 1♥-2♠. Once again, we're going to strip down the old clunker for racing purposes. By defining this type of initial jump shift response as weak, we are going to combine two essential functions into one bid:

Obstructive: we're going to take away auction space from the opponents when our responder has a weak distributional hand.

Constructive: we're going to find otherwise difficult-to-reach partscores, games and, occasionally, slams based not on pure HCP but on fits that feature a long suit in a very weak responder's hand.

How weak is it?

First of all, we're only talking about these three auctions:

You	Partner		You	Partner		You	Partner
1♣ *or* 1♦	2♥		1♣ *or* 1♦	2♠		1♥	2♠

This WJS is made on hands with a 6-card major that have no more strength than the worst weak two-bid you can imagine — and perhaps even less than that!

Surely, you are asking, there must be some quality controls? Almost none! But some practical considerations should apply:

- *No 4-card holding in the other major.*

- *2-6 HCP with some attention paid to vulnerability.*

- *The suit length is important – never five, usually six and rarely seven.*

- *The suit quality is not very important – after all, how good a suit can you have with 2-6 HCP?*

- *No more than one high card outside your long suit.*

These would be hands that would qualify for weak jump shifts:

♠ A 10 8 7 6 5　♥ J 7　♦ 7 4 2　♣ 3 2

A near-maximum.

♠ K 9　♥ Q 10 7 6 5 4　♦ 6 4　♣ 8 5 2

Another good one!

♠ Q 10 8 6 5 4　♥ Q 3　♦ 7 4 3　♣ 9 2

More the norm.

Then what happens?

Because of the very narrow limits assigned to partner's suit length and/or HCP, you will have a fairly accurate estimate of your side's prospects – both offensive and defensive.

Feel free to apply methods similar to those you already use after a weak two-bid opening always keeping in mind that in one sense, partner has already bid a lot of

your high-card values. Rebids should either be geared towards further obstruction of the opponents or should be centred around the known long suit of the WJS. With a misfit for the WJS, you shouldn't make rebids that are geared to escape from partner's suit.

Here's a scheme of possible continuations that I find works, but by all means use whatever you feel comfortable with:

1. A rebid of 2NT asks partner to show a high-card feature outside his known long suit (you probably play this already in response to weak twos). With no outside feature, but a really good suit, partner should rebid 3NT.

♠ Q 3 2 ♥ A Q 4 3 ♦ 3 ♣ A Q 9 3 2

You	Partner
1♣	2♠
2NT	

If partner has a club card or a really good suit, you will take a shot at 4♠.

2. Raising the WJS suit to the 3-level – a furtherance of the preempt, not constructive, based on a known nine-card fit.

♠ 4 3 ♥ K J 7 ♦ A K Q 5 4 ♣ 6 5 4

You	Partner
1♦	2♥
3♥	

On this hand you might wonder why the opponents haven't entered the auction yet but they're probably just about to do so. Knowing your side has little defense against a spade contract, you can make life more difficult for the opponents by raising to 3♥.

3. New suit bids by you, or rebids of your first suit, will be rare but would be made on very strong hands with little or no fit for partner's long suit. In other words, the new suit rebid should not be made out of pure fright but with some reasonable expectation of getting to a superior contract.

♠ 4 ♥ 6 ♦ A Q J 9 4 3 ♣ A K J 10 4

You	Partner
1♦	2♥
3♣	

This is a reasonable hand for a 3♣ rebid, but with

♠ K 7 ♥ 6 ♦ A J 7 6 5 ♣ K J 7 4 3

you are too weak, and should simply pass 2♥ and hope for the best.

An optional extra

In place of a 3♣ rebid over a WJS to show clubs — as shown in the example just above — some users of WJS employ this particular rebid as an artificial relay to ask partner to show any side-suit shortness (usually a singleton but occasionally a void). This is another gadget that you may already be familiar with from Weak Two-bid auctions. It can have some serious usefulness in diagnosing perfect fits for both game and slam contracts and really isn't much of a loss in a natural sense of 3♣ showing clubs, even if your opening bid was 1♣. Here is a recent systemic triumph for this approach:

Opener	Responder
♠ K J 9	♠ Q 10 7 5 4 3
♥ A 9 4	♥ 8
♦ A	♦ J 8 7
♣ A K Q 6 5 4	♣ 9 7 2
1♣	2♠
3♣	3♥
4NT	5♣
6♠	pass

After the WJS, opener's 3♣ asked for shortness in a side suit and 3♥ showed no more than one heart. Ever the optimist, opener asked for aces, prepared to bid seven on the nine-card fit, but signed off in a small slam when the spade ace was missing. This scored rather well in a team match when the other table's final contract was 1♣!

Summary

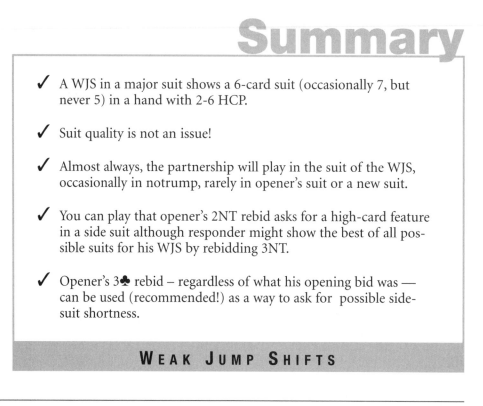

✓ A WJS in a major suit shows a 6-card suit (occasionally 7, but never 5) in a hand with 2-6 HCP.

✓ Suit quality is not an issue!

✓ Almost always, the partnership will play in the suit of the WJS, occasionally in notrump, rarely in opener's suit or a new suit.

✓ You can play that opener's 2NT rebid asks for a high-card feature in a side suit although responder might show the best of all possible suits for his WJS by rebidding 3NT.

✓ Opener's 3♣ rebid – regardless of what his opening bid was — can be used (recommended!) as a way to ask for possible side-suit shortness.

WEAK JUMP SHIFTS

NOW TRY THESE...

Yes or No, do the following hands qualify for a WJS over partner's 1♦ opening bid?

1	♠ A K 10 5 4 2	♥ 6 4 3	♦ 9 5	♣ J 8
2	♠ 9 7 6 5 3 2	♥ 5 4	♦ 10 4	♣ 4 3 2
3	♠ 10 5	♥ 8 7 6	♦ 7 2	♣ K Q J 10 4 3
4	♠ Q 10 9 5 4 3	♥ 8 7	♦ Q 3	♣ 10 5 4
5	♠ 10 9 7 6 4 3	♥ 8 7 6	♦ 9	♣ K 10 4

WJS in action! Construct an auction for each pair of hands in problems 6-14. With the suggested auction in the Answers, this time I'll include information about the entire deal since all of these samples were taken from actual competition and I know you're curious to see how all of this is going to work in real life.

6	*Opener*	*Responder*
	♠ 7	♠ J 10 8 6 4 3
	♥ A Q 8 7 6	♥ 4
	♦ K Q J 6 5	♦ 9 4 2
	♣ 8 7	♣ Q J 5

7	*Opener*	*Responder*
	♠ A Q 9	♠ K 10 7 5 4 3
	♥ 9 7	♥ 10 5 4
	♦ K Q J 8 6 5	♦ 9 3
	♣ 8 5	♣ 9 4 3

8	*Opener*	*Responder*
	♠ 9 2	♠ J 10 7 6 5 4
	♥ A Q	♥ 8 7 4
	♦ A K Q J 7 6 5	♦ 8
	♣ Q 4	♣ K 10 3

9	*Opener*	*Responder*
	♠ A 8 7 6	♠ 10 9 5 4 3 2
	♥ 9	♥ J 7 3
	♦ K Q 10 3	♦ 9 4
	♣ A K 8 2	♣ Q 9

10	*Opener*	*Responder*
	♠ K 9 7	♠ Q 10 8 6 3 2
	♥ A 5	♥ 9 6 3
	♦ A K 8 7	♦ J 4
	♣ K J 10 5	♣ 8 4

11	*Opener*	*Responder*
	♠ A J 8 5 4	♠ 10 9 7 6 3 2
	♥ 9 5 3	♥ 6
	♦ —	♦ K 10 4 3
	♣ A K Q 7 2	♣ 8 4

12	*Opener*	*Responder*
	♠ K Q 4	♠ J 10 8 7 5 2
	♥ A K Q 10 9	♥ 6 3
	♦ 7 3	♦ Q 10 8
	♣ A 10 5	♣ 9 4

13	*Opener*	*Responder*
	♠ 2	♠ K J 8 5 4 3
	♥ A K Q 5	♥ 9 3
	♦ K J 8 7	♦ 4
	♣ Q 8 7 4	♣ 10 6 5 2

14	*Opener*	*Responder*
	♠ A 8 7	♠ 9 5 4
	♥ K 8	♥ Q 9 7 5 4 3
	♦ A K J 7	♦ 9 4
	♣ Q J 8 7	♣ K 2

ANSWERS

1 No   The hand is too strong.

2 No   This hand is too weak but I have to admit that, not vulnerable, a 2♠ response is the kind of adventure that occasionally appeals to WJS addicts!

3 No   Of course not – WJS's are only made in major suits, silly!

4 Yes   A fair prototype for a WJS.

5 Yes   Just right – suit quality should not be a real issue when considering a WJS.

6

Opener	Responder
1♥[1]	2♠[2]
pass[3]	

1. Normal opening with 5-5 — open the higher-ranked suit.
2. WJS.
3. The disciplined and sensible thing to do. There's not enough compensating high card strength or extra suit length to go looking for a superior contract on this apparent misfit.

What Happened

The opponents had been frozen out of the auction although they could make ten tricks in clubs. Further, 2♠ was hard to defend accurately, and the final result was only down one. Note that a 3♦ rebid would have located a fit but a trump lead and continuation (obvious) would have produced down three!

7

Opener	Responder
1♦	2♠
3♠[1]	pass

1. The opponents must be able to make a lot of tricks in hearts and/or clubs! To make their task even more difficult, opener should make the preemptive re-raise to 3♠ and, since this is not invitational, responder should pass.

What Happened

The opponents were vulnerable versus not, and as a result were somewhat conservative in not getting into the auction sooner. They would certainly have reopened with a takeout double if opener had passed at his second turn, but the spade raise kept them out. Although 3♠ went down one trick, that was scant compensation for the sure game and possible small slam available to the non-bidders!

8

Opener	Responder
1♦	2♠
2NT[1]	3♣[2]
3NT	pass

1. Asking for a side feature.
2. Club card.

What Happened

3NT made ten tricks on a heart lead when declarer forced out the club ace at Trick 2 and the defense couldn't untangle three spade tricks.

9

Opener	Responder
1♦	2♠
4♠[1]	pass

1. There is a known 10-card fit and the heart shortness is an added asset.

What Happened

4♠ just made when trumps split 2-1 and there was no defensive ruff available with the singleton honor. Aren't you glad you weren't either defending hearts or passed out in 1♦ — frequent results when this deal was played in a Regional Pairs game?

10

Opener	Responder
1♦	2♠
4♠[1]	pass

1. The wealth of high cards looks like just enough, even not vulnerable, to give game a shot.

What Happened

As it turned out, this contract depended on declarer guessing the location of the missing club honors (assuming they were split, otherwise it wouldn't matter). However, the opening leader, with little to go on, led a club from Q976 and declarer simply played for him not to have underled an ace.

11

Opener	Responder
1♣	2♠
3♣[1]	3♥[2]
6♠[3]	pass

1. Asks for shortness.
2. Shortness in hearts.
3. Wow – a perfect fit!

What Happened

One of my favorite 'system' hands of all time! Alas, the trumps were 2-0 and a heart lead would have meant down one but the lead was actually a diamond and declarer's heart loser disappeared on the clubs just in time. You'd have to ask our opponents why they weren't in the bidding but our teammates played in five hearts, down one on a club lead.

12

Opener	Responder
1♥	2♠
4♠[1]	pass

1. No money-back guarantees but great playing strength and a known nine-card fit.

What Happened

The defense led a diamond, took two diamond tricks and forced out the club ace. However, declarer simply ran the hearts now to discard his club and the defender short in hearts could find nothing lower to ruff in with than the trump ace!

13

Opener	Responder
1♦	2♠
pass[1]	

1. With a clear misfit, pass before anything more serious develops.

What Happened

This was not a pretty contract as both the spades and diamonds were stacked over our length in those suits, so the final result was a dismal down two vulnerable. However, this turned out to be not so bad in the comparison scoring when a popular contract was one diamond passed out and down four!

14

Opener	Responder
1♦	2♥
2NT[1]	3♣[2]
3♥[3]	pass

1. Asking for a feature.
2. Club card.
3. Since the fit was only eight cards and the great heart suit opener had been hoping for hasn't been delivered, he settles for 3♥.

What Happened

Virtue was rewarded (of course!) when the defender over the strong hand held ♥AJ10 and even 3♥ was in jeopardy (but just made!).

S T E P **21**

NEW MINOR FORCING

> ♥ To know when to go ahead, when to stop, look and listen, and when to recognize the red light of danger, is to play winning Contract. *Dudley Courtenay.* **The System the Experts Play.** *1934.*

This Step covers a third gadget that I'm sure you're going to like if you don't already play it, or something like it. Using five-card major openings along with a strong notrump (usually 15-17 HCP), you will frequently have auctions that start

Partner	You
1♣ or 1♦	1♥ or 1♠
1NT	?

In Standard methods, the bid of a new suit now would not be forcing, and as a result, if you have a game-going hand, or even an invitational hand, you have to make a jump bid of some kind. Playing New Minor Forcing (NMF), the bid of a previously unbid minor suit over a 1NT rebid is forcing and artificial, simply asking partner to describe his hand further. Using this convention, after

Partner	You
1♣	1♠
1NT	?

a 2♦ rebid is artificial and forcing, while 2♣ is natural and to play.

You can also use NMF in the one auction where no minor has yet been bid:

Partner	You
1♥	1♠
1NT	?

You can either always use 2♣ as NMF here, or agree to bid your better minor.

When would I want to use this convention?

Basically, NMF is most frequently used in one of the following situations:
- *You want to find out if partner has a 3-card fit for your major (four-card support having been denied by the notrump rebid):*

  ♠ A K J 5 4   ♥ A 4   ♦ K J 7 6   ♣ 5 2

Partner	You
1♣	1♠
1NT	2♦

- *You want to check for a possible fit in the unbid major:*

  ♠ A Q 10 6 5   ♥ A 7 4 3   ♦ 8   ♣ K J 8

Partner	You
1♣	1♠
1NT	2♦

Notice that a 2♥ rebid by you shows a weak hand, and simply asks partner to pick a major at the two-level. Now you have NMF available, however, you can reserve the jump to 3♥ for a good hand with at least 5-5 shape.

- *You want to show a fit for partner's minor and make a slam try that, if rejected, won't get you past 3NT:*

  ♠ A K 5 3   ♥ A 4   ♦ K 8   ♣ K 9 5 4 3

Partner	You
1♣	1♠
1NT	2♦

Eventually you will show some slam interest based on a club fit.

- *You want to make sure you don't get to 3NT with an unstopped suit when an alternative game is available.*

  ♠ A K 5 3   ♥ A 4   ♦ 8 3 2   ♣ K 9 5 4

Partner	You
1♣	1♠
1NT	2♦

Here, the most likely game looks to be 3NT, but without a diamond stopper, you cannot bid it. So you use NMF to give partner a chance to tell you more.

Notice that in all cases, you want at least to invite game; in other words, when you use NMF, you are guaranteeing at least 11 HCP.

What do you do when partner uses NMF?

Now you know what NMF is all about, let's go back to the other side of the table. You open the bidding and rebid 1NT, and partner launches into NMF. What do you do?

In order of priority — i.e. do (1) first, if possible, then (2) and so on — your choices are to:

1) **Show 3-card support for partner's major.**

♠ Q 4 ♥ A 7 6 ♦ K Q 8 5 4 ♣ K 8 3

You	Partner
1♦	1♥
1NT	2♣
2♥	

If partner bids an invitational 3♥ now, you will go on to game.

2) **Show an unbid 4-card major.**

♠ 8 7 ♥ A Q J 7 ♦ K 7 6 5 ♣ Q J 6

You	Partner
1♦	1♠
1NT	2♣
2♥	

If partner is interested in hearts, he will raise. If what he really wants is spade support, he will probably go on in notrump.

3) **Show a good 5-card holding in your own minor.** In this context 'good' should usually be taken to mean two of the top three honors.

♠ A 8 6 ♥ 9 2 ♦ A 8 6 ♣ A Q 9 6 5

You	Partner
1♣	1♥
1NT	2♦
3♣	

4) **Rebid notrump with all unbid suits stopped.**

♠ 10 4 ♥ K Q J ♦ A Q 3 ♣ J 10 5 4 3

You	Partner
1♣	1♠
1NT	2♦
2NT	

BY THE WAY

Some writers advocate using the NMF convention only on hands with game-forcing strength. As usual, there are pros and cons to both approaches, but the method described here is far and away the most widely used.

NEW MINOR FORCING

What's the catch?

There always is one, since whenever you use a bid artificially, you lose it in its natural sense. Here's the problem hand:

♠ K 4 3 2   ♥ 3   ♦ 3 2   ♣ K 10 8 5 3 2

Partner	You
1♦	1♠
1NT	?

You can be pretty certain that 2♣ will be a better contract than 1NT, but now you can't bid it, as it would be NMF! One solution is to bid 3♣ on this type of hand, agreeing with partner that this bid means 'Leave me alone, I want to play here.' If you have a good hand with both black suits, you can start with 2♣ NMF and then rebid 3♣, so you no longer need 3♣ in this auction as a forcing bid.

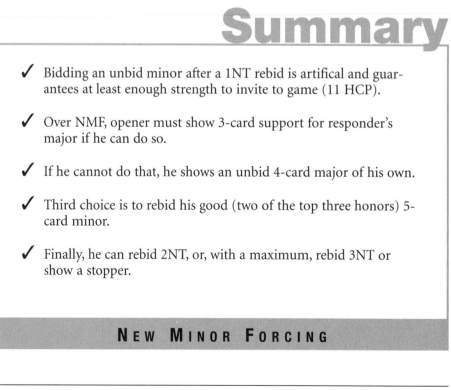

Summary

✓ Bidding an unbid minor after a 1NT rebid is artifical and guarantees at least enough strength to invite to game (11 HCP).

✓ Over NMF, opener must show 3-card support for responder's major if he can do so.

✓ If he cannot do that, he shows an unbid 4-card major of his own.

✓ Third choice is to rebid his good (two of the top three honors) 5-card minor.

✓ Finally, he can rebid 2NT, or, with a maximum, rebid 3NT or show a stopper.

NEW MINOR FORCING

NOW TRY THESE...

Try to construct the auctions on these hands, using your new NMF weapon.

1

Opener	Responder
♠ K 8 7	♠ A 9 5 4 2
♥ Q J 9	♥ A 3 2
♦ K 8 7	♦ A 9 2
♣ Q J 9 2	♣ K 4

2

Opener	Responder
♠ Q 4	♠ A K 9 5 2
♥ A J 8 7	♥ K 9 3 2
♦ Q J 5 4	♦ K 10 2
♣ K 9 3	♣ 6

3

Opener	Responder
♠ K 8 7	♠ Q 9 2
♥ 9 2	♥ A K 10 7 5
♦ A 9 3	♦ K 4
♣ A K 10 6 4	♣ Q 7 5

4

Opener	Responder
♠ Q 9 5	♠ 8 7
♥ Q 4	♥ A J 8 7
♦ K J 9 5 4	♦ 2
♣ A 9 5	♣ 10 9 8 7 6 4

5

Opener	Responder
♠ Q 7 6	♠ K J 10 4
♥ 7 6	♥ A K J 5
♦ A K 9 6 5	♦ Q 4
♣ K Q 3	♣ A J 7

ANSWERS

1

Opener	Responder
1♣	1♠
1NT	2♦[1]
2♠[2]	4♠[3]
pass	

1. NMF.
2. 3-card support.
3. Thank you.

2

Opener	Responder
1♦	1♠
1NT	2♣[1]
2♥[2]	4♥[3]
pass	

1. NMF.
2. I have four hearts without three spades.
3. Looks like the right game and that's all I was interested in exploring.

3

Opener	Responder
1♣	1♥
1NT	2♦[1]
3♣[2]	3NT[3]
pass	

1. NMF.
2. Good five-card club suit without three hearts.
3. Thanks but no thanks, let's play the obvious game.

4

Opener	Responder
1♦	1♥
1NT	3♣[1]
pass	

1. Natural and to play, with a weak hand.

5

Opener	Responder
1♦	1♥
1NT	4NT[1]
6NT[2]	pass

1. After opener's rebid, responder knows there is no suit fit worth pursuing so he invites slam in notrump with a purely quantitative raise of notrump (more about this kind of thing in my next book!).
2. Opener accepts with his maximum and good diamond suit.

INGBERMAN
OVER REVERSES

> ♥ This convention is usually misunderstood even by better players.
> **Dudley Courtenay The System the Experts Play. 1934.**

Some of the most awkward sequences in natural bidding arise after opener reverses. Just to remind you what this implies:

- *A reverse by opener is a simple rebid in a new suit which bypasses the cheapest rebid level of his first suit.*
- *A reverse promises 16+ HCP with the upper limit being just short of a hand on which you would open a game-forcing 2♣.*
- *The second-bid suit will always be shorter than the first.*
- *A reverse is forcing on responder for one round.*

The crux of the problem is that after a sequence like

Partner	You
1♦	1♠
2♥	?

there isn't a lot of auction space left for you to sort out weak hands from good hands. At the same time, you want to be able to agree on a suit and possibly conduct some slam exploration below game.

BY THE WAY

Some writers lump the treatment we're about to explore in with the 'Lebensohl' convention. However, Lebensohl is a more recent development and not really the same thing. Besides, there are enough other applications of Lebensohl around so it'll at least help avoid confusion if we attribute our variety of the reverse solution gadget to Ingberman.

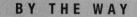

A reverse, as we have seen, is a one-round force – you cannot pass. But many times, when you have made a first response on minimal values, you will be terrified of bidding again (been there, haven't you?) lest partner get over-exuberant with his known-to-be-good hand (don't they always?). Other times, you will have quite a good hand and, unsure of what is forcing and what isn't, either plant the partnership in 3NT (frequently too low or just plain wrong) or launch into the stratosphere via Blackwood (almost always wrong and/or too high). None of these results is likely to be satisfactory.

So what's the answer?

Monroe Ingberman, one of the great American bridge theorists of the sixties (and later), tackled this problem and his highly original solution is the one I recommend to handle reverses.

Here again is a typical reverse sequence:

Partner	You
1♣	1♠
2♥	?

Generally speaking, with any hand that is so weak as to be unlikely to produce game opposite partner's minimum hand for a reverse (16 HCP, 5-4 shape), you rebid 2NT.

BY THE WAY

The one exception you might make to this is that rebidding your own 5+card major suit at the two-level is not forcing. That's up to you and your partner to discuss and agree.

This 2NT rebid **orders** partner to bid 3♣ (whatever his original suit was) and pass your next bid, whatever it is. You may even be intending to pass his 3♣ bid (with clubs!) if you don't want to get any higher. It follows that anything you bid over partner's reverse other than 2NT creates a game force. If you do bid something other than 2NT, all our usual Two-over-One implications follow, including going slowly with strong hands and Fast Arrival on hands with no slam interest.

Keep in mind that:

• The 2NT rebid is artificial – *it doesn't necessarily show any inclination to play in notrump!*

• While partner promised 16 HCP as a minimum, he could have considerably more and you are basing your bidding on the likelihood of partner having no more than a minimum.

• Accordingly, partner's usual course of action will be to obey and bid 3♣; **but** (there's always a 'but' isn't there?)...

• Partner may **disobey** (i.e. bid something other than 3♣) if he's so strong that he thinks there should be a good play for game even opposite your possible minimum. His extra strength may be in HCP or distributional playing

strength but he shouldn't take disobedience lightly –
you will frequently have very little of use.

- The form partner's 'disobedience' should take will
usually be fairly obvious to him – i.e. bid notrump
with the unbid suit stopped, or continue to show his
pattern by supporting your suit or showing extra
length in one or both of his suits.

Ingberman 2NT in action

Let's a look at some examples of how this works in practice.

Opener	Responder
♠ 8 2	♠ Q 9 5 4
♥ A K Q 3	♥ 8 2
♦ A K J 6 2	♦ Q 9 4
♣ 7 2	♣ Q 9 4 3
1♦	1♠
2♥[1]	2NT[2]
3♣[3]	3♦[4]
pass[5]	

1. Reverse, 16+ HCP, forcing one round, longer diamonds than hearts.
2. Please bid 3♣ – I may not have much!
3. Obeying – a minimum reverse.
4. Here's where I want to play. Thank goodness, I'm out of this auction with my life!
5. Sigh.

Opener	Responder
♠ 8 2	♠ Q J 7 6 5
♥ A K Q 3	♥ J 10 4 2
♦ A K J 6 2	♦ 8
♣ 7 2	♣ Q J 8
1♦	1♠
2♥	2NT[1]
3♣[2]	3♥[3]
pass[4]	

1. Please bid 3♣.
2. Obedience with a minimum reverse.
3. A fit but not enough for game unless you have something extra (responder could have bid a direct 3♥ or 4♥ with four hearts and enough for game).
4. I certainly have nothing that I haven't already shown.

Opener	Responder
♠ 9	♠ Q J 8 4
♥ A J 10 3	♥ 9 8 2
♦ A K Q 10 2	♦ 9 7 3
♣ A Q 9	♣ K 8 4
1♦	1♠
2♥	2NT[1]
3NT[2]	pass

1. Please rebid 3♣ so I can bid 3♦ — I don't have a very good hand.
2. Disobedience with substantial extra values and the unbid suit stopped, certainly enough to play game after responder showed 6+ HCP with his first response.

Opener	Responder
♠ A Q J 8 7	♠ 9 2
♥ A K Q 8 5 4	♥ J 6
♦ K 7	♦ Q 8 5 4
♣ —	♣ Q J 8 7 4
1♥	1NT
2♠	2NT[1]
3♠[2]	4♥[3]
pass	

1. Please rebid 3♣ with a minimum so I can drop you in 3♥.
2. Disobedience showing five spades and six hearts (at least) and a game force opposite a minimum 1NT (which was forcing, remember?).
3. Okay, I pick hearts.

Summary

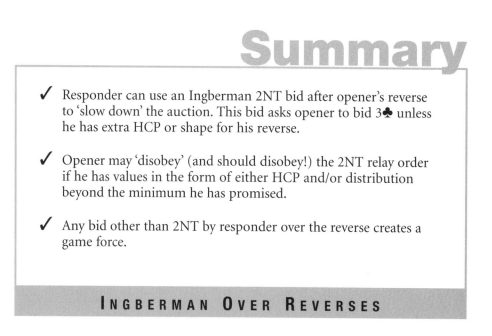

✓ Responder can use an Ingberman 2NT bid after opener's reverse to 'slow down' the auction. This bid asks opener to bid 3♣ unless he has extra HCP or shape for his reverse.

✓ Opener may 'disobey' (and should disobey!) the 2NT relay order if he has values in the form of either HCP and/or distribution beyond the minimum he has promised.

✓ Any bid other than 2NT by responder over the reverse creates a game force.

INGBERMAN OVER REVERSES

NOW TRY THESE...

What is your next bid in each case?

1
♠ K Q 9 2
♥ 9 4 2
♦ 5 4 3
♣ J 10 2

Partner	You
1♦	1♠
2♥	?

2
♠ K J 8 4
♥ 8 4
♦ J 9 6 5
♣ A 8 6

Partner	You
1♦	1♠
2♥	?

3
♠ K Q 9 4 3 2
♥ 9 4
♦ J 8 3
♣ 10 9

Partner	You
1♣	1♠
2♥	?

4
♠ K 10 9 4 3
♥ 9 5
♦ J 7
♣ A 8 7 2

Partner	You
1♦	1♠
2♥	?

5
♠ Q 8 7 6
♥ 7 5
♦ 10 4 2
♣ K J 8 4

Partner	You
1♦	1♠
2♥	?

6
♠ 6
♥ A K Q 6 5
♦ A K Q J 7 2
♣ 9

You	Partner
1♦	1♠
2♥	2NT
?	

7
♠ 7
♥ Q J 10 2
♦ A K Q 4 3
♣ K Q 4

You	Partner
1♦	1♠
2♥	2NT
?	

8
♠ 8 7
♥ A Q 10 2
♦ K 7
♣ A K J 7 6

You	Partner
1♣	1♠
2♥	2NT
?	

9
♠ K 10 3
♥ A Q J 10
♦ A K J 7 6
♣ 9

You	Partner
1♣	1♠
2♥	2NT
?	

10
♠ 9
♥ A K J 10
♦ A K Q 9 6 5 3
♣ Q

You	Partner
1♦	1♠
2♥	2NT
	?

ANSWERS

1 2NT   You will sign off in 3♦ unless partner shows something extra.

2 3♦   For now just tell partner about your diamond support. Remember that this is game-forcing since you didn't go through Ingberman 2NT.

3 2NT   You intend to rebid 3♠ and play there. If you play 2♠ as non-forcing, you would bid this instead. Also, if you play WJS (Step 20), you would have bid 2♠ in the first place and got this hand off your chest!

4 2♠   Natural and forward-going (unless you've agreed it isn't, in which case use the 2NT gadget here and rebid 3♠).

5 2NT   You'll get out in 3♦ unless partner has extras.

6 3♥   Much too much to obey partner and bid 3♣ – he might be planning to pass! Your rebid promises five hearts, and therefore at least six diamonds.

7 3♣   A good hand, but not enough to force to game opposite a 6-count.

8 3♣   Again, a good hand, but not enough to force to game opposite a 6-count. Discipline!

9 3♠   Too much to go quietly with 3♣ this time, especially with the spade fit. If partner has five spades, you must be a favorite to make 4♠.

10 4♦   A strong hand with lots of diamonds – a simple, natural bid.

S T E P

23

OVER A TAKEOUT DOUBLE

♥ Bank on probabilities. The bank may suspend, but it will not fail.
Criticus. **Contract Simplicitas.** *1933.*

When our side has opened the bidding with one of a suit and an opponent makes a takeout double, it takes absolutely no auction space away from us and, indeed, gives us one more word in our bidding language ('redouble') that we wouldn't have otherwise.

Thus, it is theoretically possible essentially to ignore the double and continue bidding just as if it hadn't happened, and many pairs do just that. Sadly, this simple (perhaps simplistic!) approach to bidding only works as long as the next opponent doesn't follow his partner's lead into the bidding fray! A more aware approach takes into account that the doubler has shown an opening bid and has invited his partner to contest the auction in one of the unbid suits – an invitation that seemingly gets accepted these days with ever-diminishing justification for so doing!

How are major-suit auctions different?

As you will have found in your own experience, the most significant loss of bidding space and potential accuracy occurs due to actions by the doubler's partner. Accordingly, responder is frequently not going to have the luxury of being able to take two low-level actions to describe his hand. For instance, with

♠ Q J 7 ♥ K 8 7 6 ♦ 5 2 ♣ 8 7 3 2

in an uncontested auction responder could show a weak raise of a major by first responding 1NT (forcing) and then raising or giving preference to opener's first-bid major at his second turn. This would be a typical auction:

Partner	You
1♠	1NT
2♣	2♠

However, if instead the auction unfolds as follows:

Partner	Oppt.	You	Oppt.
1♠	dbl	1NT	3♥
pass	pass	?	

you are in a trickier situation. You don't have either the values or the trumps to bid 3♠ now. On the other hand, if partner had known you had spade support, he might have bid more himself – but he didn't. To compete effectively over fourth hand's anticipated bid of a new suit, partner will often need to know about our 3-card fit. Thus one of the most significant changes we should make after a takeout double is to include the weak raise variety of supporting hand into our parameters for a single raise.

So, now this auction

Partner	Oppt.	You	Oppt.
1♠	dbl	2♠	

will show 6-9 HCP with either 3- or 4-card support for partner (more or less like Standard except that, if you're at the upper end of your range, you will not have four cards in support as you can still make a Bergen 3♣ raise with that hand).

The other immediate raises of opener's major — 3♣ or 3♦ as Bergen raises, 2NT as a forcing Jacoby raise or three of the major as a preemptive raise — need not be changed at this juncture; however, you should keep in mind that the frequency of a game-forcing raise will be somewhat less in light of the opponent's announced strength.

What about a redouble?

Although the seemingly innocent takeout double does take away some of our comfort in constructive bidding, it does give us back a little by allowing us to redouble. I'll deal with redouble auctions (which can get very complex) in greater depth in my next book but, for now, this almost-Standard set of parameters works well:

Partner	Oppt.	You	Oppt.
1♥ or 1♠	dbl	redbl	

You start with a redouble on all hands with 10+ HCP except for:

- *A forcing raise (Jacoby 2NT)*

- *A limit raise (3♦)*

So you will redouble with all other 10+ hands, including

- *Supporting hands with 10-12 HCP (or more) and only three trumps*

- *Hands that would normally bid a natural game-forcing Two-over-One response*

- *Hands with 10-12 HCP without a fit that normally would bid a Forcing 1NT and follow up to show invitational values.*

After responder has redoubled, your current practices (assuming you have some) should be fine for the time being as long as you realize that:

- Redouble followed by a new suit bid by responder is forcing – for at least one round and maybe to game depending on the follow-up.

- Redouble followed by the appropriate-level raise of opener's major shows the 10-12 HCP hand with 3-card support.

- Redouble followed by a cuebid of the opponents' suit shows a 3-card fit with 12+ HCP.

- You should not let the opponents play undoubled at the two-level after a redouble by your side. If you don't want to defend, bid something!

Are there any other changes?

With all strong hands after major-suit openings now accounted for, we can change the meaning of both our 1NT response and our natural Two-over-One response.

First, a 1NT response after a takeout double no longer need be forcing, so it will be more like an old-fashioned Standard 1NT – 6-9 HCP without support for opener's major. Further bidding by opener should follow natural lines with the need to rebid a 3-card suit no longer in effect.

As well, with the availability of the redouble to show strong hands (and the takeout double making it somewhat less likely that responder will have great strength), we can also change the meaning of our Two-over-One response. This can now be made with a hand that has:

- *A good suit – usually 6+ cards in length*
- *Less than 10 HCP*
- *No real fit for opener's suit since there is no intention to keep the auction forcing*

So that after

Partner	Oppt.	You	Oppt.
1♠	dbl	?	

you can bid 2♦ with

♠ 8 ♥ K 8 7 ♦ K J 10 9 5 4 ♣ 10 5 4

What about minor-suit auctions?

Partner	Oppt.	You	Oppt.
1♣ or 1♦	dbl	?	

All of your 'weaker' responses (single raise, 1NT and WJS) to minor-suit openings can remain unchanged after the takeout double. Similarly, your one-over-one responses can remain unchanged, although of course with a minimum in both points and length, you should not feel forced to act at all. Just as was the case in major-suit auctions, you no longer need play the Two-over-One sequence

Partner	Oppt.	You	Oppt.
1♦	dbl	2♣	

as game-forcing, since you can start with a redouble on good hands. The simplest way to play it is much the same as it would be after a major-suit opening is doubled for takeout – long clubs with less than 10 HCP, non-forcing.

The other initial strength-showing responses after a minor opening has been doubled will be the area where some modification can be beneficial. Because of the interference, our strategy has been affected somewhat:

- we may have the opportunity to secure a penalty
- we may want to take advantage of a significant minor suit fit to preempt the opponents or to sacrifice
- we'll almost surely have less room for constructive bidding.

This is one effective scheme to address those strategic concerns:

- 3 of opener's minor: still the same limit raise it was without the double.
- 2NT: a preemptive raise of opener's minor. When holding a balanced 11-12 HCP hand, start by redoubling rather than with 2NT.
- Use the jump shift in the other minor to show a weak, preemptive style hand. Criss-Cross minor forcing raises are not only less likely to come up after the takeout double but can be described after an initial redouble.

Summary

	NO DOUBLE	OVER A TAKEOUT DOUBLE
AFTER MAJOR OPENINGS		
single raise	7-10 HCP, 3-card support	6-9 HCP, 3- or 4-card support
dbl raise	preemptive	unchanged
3♣, 3♦	Bergen raises	unchanged
2NT	Jacoby forcing raise	unchanged
1NT	5-12 HCP forcing 1 round may have support for opener	6-9 HCP non-forcing no support
2♣, 2♦ and 2♥ (over 1♠)	natural, game forcing opening bid+	natural, nonforcing 9 HCP or less
redouble	not available	10+ HCP except as above (3♦ or 2NT types)
AFTER MINOR OPENINGS		
1-over-1	4+cards, 6+ HCP forcing one round	unchanged, except should be reluctant to bid with minimum
WJS	6+ cards, 6 HCP or less	unchanged
1NT	6-9 HCP, no major	unchanged non-forcing
2NT	11-12 HCP, game-invitational	preemptive raise of opener's minor
dbl raise	limit raise, 10-12 HCP, 5+card support	unchanged
3♣ over 1♦ 2♦ over 1♣	Criss-Cross artificial forcing raise	natural, less than 10 HCP, non-forcing
2♣ over 1♦	natural Two-over-One Game Force	natural, non-forcing more balanced than 3♣
single raise	6-9 HCP 5+ card support	same but not enough shape to preempt

NOW TRY THESE...

Pick your response to partner's indicated opening bid in each case:

1
- ♠ K J 8 7
- ♥ Q 4 3
- ♦ 8 7
- ♣ 10 6 4 3

Partner	Oppt.	You	Oppt.
1♠	pass	?	

2
- ♠ K J 8 7
- ♥ Q 4 3
- ♦ 8 7
- ♣ 10 6 4 3

Partner	Oppt.	You	Oppt.
1♠	dbl	?	

3
- ♠ K J 8 7
- ♥ Q 4 3
- ♦ 8 7
- ♣ 10 6 4 3

Partner	Oppt.	You	Oppt.
1♦	pass	?	

4
- ♠ K J 8 7
- ♥ Q 4 3
- ♦ 8 7
- ♣ 10 6 4 3

Partner	Oppt.	You	Oppt.
1♦	dbl	?	

5
- ♠ 5 4
- ♥ A Q 4 3
- ♦ K Q 9 4
- ♣ J 9 6

Partner	Oppt.	You	Oppt.
1♠	pass	?	

6
- ♠ 5 4
- ♥ A Q 4 3
- ♦ K Q 9 4
- ♣ J 9 6

Partner	Oppt.	You	Oppt.
1♠	dbl	?	

7
- ♠ 5 4
- ♥ A Q 4 3
- ♦ K Q 9 4
- ♣ J 9 6

Partner	Oppt.	You	Oppt.
1♦	pass	?	

8
- ♠ 5 4
- ♥ A Q 4 3
- ♦ K Q 9 4
- ♣ J 9 6

Partner	Oppt.	You	Oppt.
1♦	dbl	?	

9
- ♠ 9
- ♥ K 7 4
- ♦ 6 4 2
- ♣ K Q 10 6 5 4

Partner	Oppt.	You	Oppt.
1♠	pass	?	

10
- ♠ 9
- ♥ K 7 4
- ♦ 6 4 2
- ♣ K Q 10 6 5 4

Partner	Oppt.	You	Oppt.
1♠	dbl	?	

11
- ♠ 9
- ♥ K 7 4
- ♦ 6 4 2
- ♣ K Q 10 6 5 4

Partner	Oppt.	You	Oppt.
1♦	pass	?	

12
- ♠ 9
- ♥ K 7 4
- ♦ 6 4 2
- ♣ K Q 10 6 5 4

Partner	Oppt.	You	Oppt.
1♦	dbl	?	

13 ♠ 8
♥ K J 9 2
♦ A Q J 10 2
♣ K 8 4

Partner	Oppt.	You	Oppt.
1♠	pass	?	

14 ♠ 8
♥ K J 9 2
♦ A Q J 10 2
♣ K 8 4

Partner	Oppt.	You	Oppt.
1♠	dbl	?	

15 ♠ 8
♥ K J 9 2
♦ A Q J 10 2
♣ K 8 4

Partner	Oppt.	You	Oppt.
1♦	pass	?	

16 ♠ 8
♥ K J 9 2
♦ A Q J 10 2
♣ K 8 4

Partner	Oppt.	You	Oppt.
1♦	dbl	?	

17 ♠ K J 7 6
♥ 6 2
♦ A Q 4 3
♣ 10 4 2

Partner	Oppt.	You	Oppt.
1♠	pass	?	

18 ♠ K J 7 6
♥ 6 2
♦ A Q 4 3
♣ 10 4 2

Partner	Oppt.	You	Oppt.
1♠	dbl	?	

19 ♠ K J 7 6
♥ 6 2
♦ A Q 4 3
♣ 10 4 2

Partner	Oppt.	You	Oppt.
1♦	pass	?	

20 ♠ K J 7 6
♥ 6 2
♦ A Q 4 3
♣ 10 4 2

Partner	Oppt.	You	Oppt.
1♦	dbl	?	

ANSWERS

1	1NT	Forcing one round, weak raise will be shown on next round.
2	2♠	6-9 HCP, 3- or 4-card support.
3	1♠	Natural 1-over-1 up the line response.
4	Pass	Discretion is the better part of valor (sometimes!).
5	1NT	Forcing 1 round.
6	Redbl	I smell blood and I hope it's theirs!
7	1♥	Natural 1-over-1, forcing one round.
8	Redbl	If you don't bid 1♥ here, you may lose a heart fit to the opponents' possible spade bidding, while if you don't redouble you may have a hard time convincing partner you have this much strength. On balance, with a queen more than a minimum, go ahead and redouble and hope the hearts look after themselves!
9	1NT	Forcing 1 round.
10	2♣	Natural and non-forcing.
11	1NT	No other choice, as you're too weak for a game-forcing 2♣.
12	3♣	Preemptive — put it to them!
13	2♦	Natural and game-forcing.
14	Redbl	10+ HCP, possibly heading for penalty versus opponents.
15	1♥	Natural 1-over-1 up the line response.
16	Redbl	Similar to Problem 8 but with substantial extra strength this time and a strain to go to (diamonds) if all else fails.
17	3♦	A Bergen limit raise.
18	3♦	A Bergen limit raise.
19	1♠	Natural 1-over-1 up the line response.
20	1♠	Not enough overall strength to plan to redouble and introduce spades later on as that would be forcing.

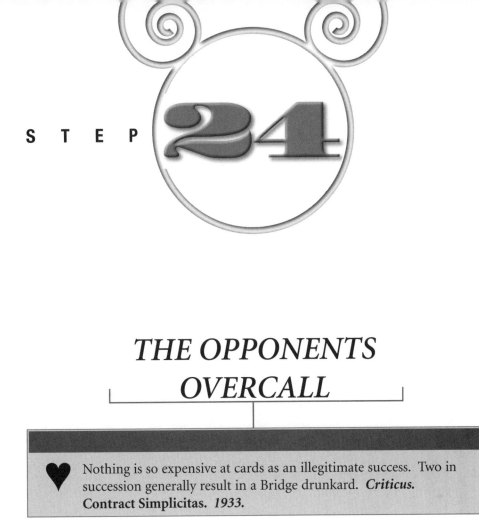

THE OPPONENTS OVERCALL

♥ Nothing is so expensive at cards as an illegitimate success. Two in succession generally result in a Bridge drunkard. *Criticus.* **Contract Simplicitas. 1933.**

While an opponent's takeout double causes only minimal immediate loss of bidding space, the same cannot be said for an overcall. Virtually all of our carefully crafted systemic agreements are laid waste by the simplest of overcalls because we suddenly just don't have the auction space we need for careful description and/or exploration. If science and accuracy can be our twin goals in an unobstructed auction, survival often becomes the issue after an overcall.

Among other things, after a major-suit opening and any overcall:

- *we can no longer use 1NT as a one-round force*

- *we cannot distinguish as many types of supporting hands*

- *natural notrump bids will guarantee stopper(s) in their suit*

Fortunately, although the overcall definitely causes us problems, it also provides some of the solutions. After the overcall, we now have two calls not previously available that we will put to good use:

- *a double of the overcall by responder*

- *a direct cuebid of overcaller's suit by responder*

Doubling the overcall

Partner	Oppt.	You	Oppt.
1♦	2♣	dbl	

Current practice is to use the immediate double of a natural suit overcall as a 'negative' double to show competitive values plus support for unbid suits, in particular support for any unbid major suit(s). Also, in line with our desire to distinguish 3-card raises from four or more, I recommend you start with a negative double when you have 10-12 HCP and 3-card support for partner's major.

Negative doubles and the auctions that follow them are involved topics, and I certainly don't have the space here to cover them in depth. Any book on competitive bidding discusses them, two books in this series do so: *25 Bridge Conventions You Should Know* and *25 Ways to Compete in the Bidding*, both by Barbara Seagram and Marc Smith.

Cuebidding their suit

The second tool the overcall has given us is a direct cuebid of the overcaller's suit.

Partner	Oppt.	You	Oppt.
1♠	2♣	3♣	

This we will use to show a raise of opener's major with at least limit raise (10+ HCP) values and at least 4-card support. Partner should proceed on the assumption that you are limited to 10-12 HCP and your follow-up can correct this (by bidding on when he signs off, for example).

Other changes

My recommendations are that some things to stay the same, while others perforce will change:

- **Single, preemptive and direct game raises** stay the same as they are over an opponent's takeout double.

- **Bergen three-level raises** are scrapped.

- **New suit bids by responder are natural,** generally 5+ cards (anything less would tend to be handled by an initial negative double) in length and show enough values for the level the bid occurs at (10+ at the two-level, 12+ at the three-level, etc). Generally, these new suit bids by responder are forcing for only one round but the level might convert that to a game force out of necessity (for example, 1♠-3♦-4♣ would effectively be a game force.)

- **Notrump responses** show 11-12 HCP at the two-level and 13-15 HCP at the three-level and most assuredly have at least one stopper in the opponent's overcalled suit.

Effect of an overcall on your bidding agreements

AFTER A MAJOR-SUIT OPENING

	NO OVERCALL	OVERCALL
Single raise	7-10 HCP 3-card support	6-10 HCP 3-4 card support
Double raise	preemptive	unchanged
Triple raise	direct game raise 5+ trumps, less than 10 HCP, some shape	unchanged
3♣, 3♦	Bergen raises	may be natural or cuebid depending on overcaller's suit
1NT	5-12 HCP, forcing	natural
2NT	Jacoby forcing raise of major	11-12 HCP, natural invitational, over- called suit stopped
3NT	15-17 HCP balanced	13-15 HCP, oppo- nent's suit stopped
Double	unavailable	negative double: competitive values with support for unbid suits, or 3-card limit raise of opener's major.
Cuebid	unavailable	limit raise or better of opener's suit with at least 4-card support.

AFTER A MINOR-SUIT OPENING

- **Natural bids** are forcing one round and usually promise 5+cards.
- **Negative doubles** show support for unbid suits, particularly unbid majors.
- **Cuebids** show a limit raise of opener's minor (5+card support) with a minimum of 10 HCP.
- **Jump raises** of the minor (a serious change!) are now best used as preemptive raises.
- **Bids of 1NT, 2NT and 3NT** show 6-9, 11-12 and 13-15 HCP respectively with stopper(s) in the overcaller's suit absolutely guaranteed.

Summary

✓ The most dramatic condition we must accommodate after an overcall is the loss of auction space. Keep in mind that the partner of the overcaller may be about to diminish our supply of space even further!

✓ We do recover some of the lost space by having negative doubles and direct cuebids made available by the overcall.

✓ Notrump bids should always show stopper(s) in the overcaller's suit.

✓ Stay tuned for more help in this context in my next book!

THE OPPONENTS OVERCALL

NOW TRY THESE...

What is your next bid with each of the following hands?

1 ♠ A Q 5 4
♥ K Q 3
♦ 8 7 6 5
♣ 10 3

Partner	Oppt.	You	Oppt.
1♠	pass	?	

2 ♠ A Q 5 4
♥ K Q 3
♦ 8 7 6 5
♣ 10 3

Partner	Oppt.	You	Oppt.
1♠	2♦	?	

3 ♠ Q 3
♥ K J 10 2
♦ 5 4 3
♣ A J 7 6

Partner	Oppt.	You	Oppt.
1♠	pass	?	

4 ♠ Q 3
♥ K J 10 2
♦ 5 4 3
♣ A J 7 6

Partner	Oppt.	You	Oppt.
1♠	2♦	?	

5 ♠ 5 4
♥ K J 7
♦ K J 7 6
♣ K 10 3 2

Partner	Oppt.	You	Oppt.
1♠	pass	?	

6 ♠ 5 4
♥ K J 7
♦ K J 7 6
♣ K 10 3 2

Partner	Oppt.	You	Oppt.
1♠	2♦	?	

7 ♠ 6
♥ A 7 6
♦ K Q J 9 3
♣ J 10 5 3

Partner	Oppt.	You	Oppt.
1♠	pass	?	

8 ♠ 6
♥ A 7 6
♦ K Q J 9 3
♣ J 10 5 3

Partner	Oppt.	You	Oppt.
1♠	2♦	?	

9 ♠ A K 8 4
♥ K 7
♦ 9 6 5 4
♣ A Q 3

Partner	Oppt.	You	Oppt.
1♠	pass	?	

10 ♠ A K 8 4
♥ K 7
♦ 9 6 5 4
♣ A Q 3

Partner	Oppt.	You	Oppt.
1♠	2♦	?	

ANSWERS

1   3♦   A 4-card limit raise of spades with 10-12 HCP.

2   3♦   Also to show a limit raise via a cuebid. Note this neither promises nor delivers a control in diamonds.

3   1NT   A one-round force.

4   Dbl   A negative double showing competitive values and support for the unbid suits — most particularly hearts, the unbid major in this auction.

5   1NT   A one-round force.

6   2NT   11-12 HCP, natural and invitational with diamonds stopped. While you might pass and seek an eventual penalty (see Problem 8) your diamond length is a little suspect for that action — but it could work out!

7   1NT   A one-round force.

8   Pass   This is the type of hand you love to hold when they've overcalled. In line with negative double practices, you're hoping your partner can reopen the auction with double (for takeout) and you will pass for penalties, blood (theirs) and pleasure (yours).

9   2NT   A Jacoby forcing raise of spades.

10   3♦   Initially showing at least a limit raise of spades, an impression you will correct subject to how the rest of the auction unfolds. For the time being, partner will at least know of the fit if not the total strength of your hand.